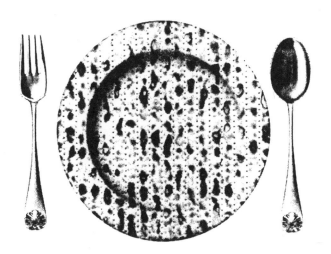

The New

KOSHER *for* PASSOVER
COOKBOOK

Revised and Expanded

AISH HATORAH
WOMEN'S ORGANIZATION

FELDHEIM PUBLISHERS
JERUSALEM · NEW YORK

Aish HaTorah
College of Jewish Studies

This cookbook is a project of Jewel — Jewish Women's
Education League and Aish HaTorah Women's Organization

See pages 135–140 for a brief glimpse at our activities.

Editors:
Rena Novack
Dvorah Eisenbach
Zelda Goldsfield

ISBN 0-87306-863-7
First published 1978
Second revised edition 1980
Third edition 1987
Fourth revised edition 1998

Feldheim Publishers
POB 35002
Jerusalem, Israel 91350

200 Airport Executive Park
Nanuet, NY 10954

Printed in Israel

Contents

V

Editor's Introduction to Fourth Edition

What's there to eat on Passover? Potatoes, potatoes and more potatoes, or so we think.

Well, surprise! The Yeshivat Aish HaTorah Women's Organization has put together just the cookbook for you! With over 250 great recipes for delightfully delectable Pesach dishes, you can try out different ones year after year, without repeating.

Our cookbook was first published in 1978 and again in 1980 and 1987. Since the first and subsequent editions have sold out, another generation has grown up. My little girl and cooking assistant took this cookbook with her when she got married, and now it's her child spilling lemon juice all over it's pages. Now that's what I call tradition!

We've added about 50 new recipes to this revised edition, including vegetarian, low cholesterol, and salt-free ones.

It used to be that Pesach meant preparing everything from scratch. My, how things have changed! Today, our opportunities have expanded from a small "Kosher for Passover" section, to special outlets handling only Pesach foods — so great is the selection. All non-*chametz* ingredients can be bought there.

But the best ingredient of all is the love and effort that each of us puts into making Pesach the gift of a lasting memory, to carry us and our loved ones through the years. We hope you'll enjoy this new, revised edition. And yes, I think this time I'll put some copies aside for the grandchildren. You live and learn.

A happy and kosher Pesach to you all!

Rena Novack
Editor
Jerusalem 5758 (1998)

Dare to Care
A Message from the Rosh HaYeshivah

It was the turn of the century and Rav Chaskel Sarne, Rosh HaYeshivah from Chevron, was at a *simchah* with the aristocracy of the Jewish People. Chassidim, Misnagdim — they all came.

When Rav Sarne approached the podium to speak, he stunned the audience by declaring, "Everyone in this room thinks that it was their grandfather or great grandfather who did the most for the Jewish People in the last 200 years. I'm here to tell you that it wasn't!" The audience was shocked — from the grandson of the Chofetz Chaim to the great grandson of the Gerrer Rebbe.

"And furthermore," Rav Sarne continued, "the person who did the most for the Jewish People in the last 200 years never even learned one page of Gemara." The crowd was astounded.

"And I'll tell you something more," said Rav Sarne, "when you hear his name, you will agree with me." And when he did, they did. Everyone agreed. The old, the young, the Chassidim and the Misnagdim.

His name — actually her name — was Sara Schneirer, founder of the Beis Yaakov school for women. Sara Schneirer, who was never educated in a school, recognized that educating women at home wasn't working anymore. While the boys in Poland were turning into *talmidei chachamim*, the girls were Communists! If she had not taken it upon herself to organize a new form of education for girls, who knows what state the Jewish People would be in today.

What made this woman a leader of such importance is clear. And today, although everyone cares about the problems facing the Jewish People: the hatred among ourselves, alienation, assimilation, intermarriage...what are we doing for our people? Although everyone cared about what was happening to the Jewish girls in Poland, only Sara Schneirer dared to take action.

Our job at Aish HaTorah is to get people to focus on how much they really care about these problems. Then we encourage everyone to feel strongly enough so they will commit their time and energy to making a difference. How? By simply showing them that they can.

An apt analogy is that almost everyone wants to become a millionaire. If someone won a lotto worth millions of dollars, he certainly would not turn it down. However, very few people strain themselves to become millionaires. Yet, there was a time in American history when hundreds of people traveled across the United States, through Indian territories, and enduring hardship and hunger to become millionaires. Why? It was the Gold Rush of 1849 and people thought there was gold lying around for the taking.

The way we produce leadership today is to show our students and anyone else who will listen that there is gold for the taking, Jewish gold. There are even diamonds, if you will, precious gems waiting to be found.

When you see it can be done, despite the hardship, when you see how feasible it is, then your caring automatically leads to action. This action leads to change and to becoming the type of leader Sara Schneirer was, a true model for each and every one of us.

Special Cooking Hints

A mixture of 1/2 matzah meal and 1/2 potato starch simulates the flavor of regular flour.

Make matzah cake meal by grinding matzah meal.

When baking with matzah meal, the baking time is shorter because the matzah meal has already been baked.

Equivalents:
1 oz. (1 square) cooking chocolate = 4 T. cocoa and 1/2 T. oil
1 lemon = 3-4 T. juice
1 orange = 6-8 T. juice

You can make confectioner's sugar by putting granulated sugar through a blender.

Using a wonder pot is a good way to bake for Pesach if you don't kasher your oven.

Check if an egg is fresh by shaking it next to your ear. Stale eggs make a rattling sound.

Give a special touch to a fruit centerpiece by adding frosted fruits or frosted grapes. Beat egg whites slightly. Dip in clusters of grapes or other small fruits — cherries, etc. Sprinkle with granulated sugar and refrigerate. When egg white hardens, the fruits are frosted.

Blanch almonds by pouring boiling water over them. After 5-10 minutes, the skins will come off very easily.

Special Note:
When a product with proper certification (*hechsher*) is not available locally, use your imagination and try a variation.

Abbreviations

T. = tablespoon(s)   oz. = ounce(s)
tsp. = teaspoon(s)   K. = kilogram(s)
lb. = pound(s)   g. = gram(s)

Checking for Insects

Insects and their larvae can be found in many different types of foods. They infest not only leafy vegetables, but also legumes, nuts, dried fruits, flour (and matzah meal!) fruits, vegetables and even fish. Different insects are attracted to different foods. Although some insects are as large as a worm in an apple, others are smaller than the head of a pin. Different countries and food production methods affect the degree of infestation.

Since several popular as well as several very technical books have been written on this subject, you should take advantage of them to study the subject carefully. Consult your local Rabbinical authority with any questions you have.

Today some leafy vegetables may be purchased pre-checked or cultivated in a bug-free manner. However, they are not always available year-round and in all locations. In our Pesach recipes, we urge you to take particular care with leafy vegetables and dried fruits.

There are seven separate Torah injunctions forbidding the ingestion of insects, so BE CAREFUL and have a happy and kosher Pesach!

Pesach Preparations

The Torah forbids eating *chametz*, benefiting from *chametz* or even possessing *chametz* during Pesach.

What is *chametz*?

Chametz is the result of fermentation initiated by water in contact with any of the five species of grain: wheat, rye, spelt, barley and oats. This means that not only are cakes, cookies and breads *chametz*, but also many alcoholic beverages — for example: beer and grain whiskey. (Grain vinegar is *chametz* as well.)

What else is forbidden to eat on Pesach?

All *Ashkenazim* refrain from eating *kitniyos* on Pesach. This includes peas, beans, lentils, mustard, rice and corn, whether fresh or dried. Many also refrain from eating peanuts and peanut oil.

Anything else?

Yes. Anything that has any *chametz* mixed with it is also forbidden. This includes many types of dried fruits and processed foods, as well as many medicines. BECAUSE OF THE MANY QUESTIONS INVOLVED IN THE USE OF EACH PRODUCT, IT IS CORRECT TO USE ONLY GOODS THAT HAVE PROPER RABBINICAL CERTIFICATION (*HECHSHER*).

Some families, especially those whose roots are Chassidic, do not eat *gebrokts*. What is that?

In Yiddish, *gebrokts* — or *matzah shruyah* in Hebrew — is matzah soaked in water or soup. In this cookbook, recipes that use matzah or matzah meal are designated with an asterisk (*), for those who don't eat *gebrokts*.

To avoid the prohibition against possessing *chametz*, areas in the home where *chametz* could possibly be found must be inspected thoroughly, and all *chametz* removed.

Mechiras Chametz (sale of *chametz*): When destruction of *chametz* would involve a significant loss of money (e.g., bottles of whiskey), Halachah allows for its inclusion in a general sale of *chametz* to a non-Jew. A local Rabbinical authority could help you determine which *chametz* products should be disposed of and what could be sold, and he will be able to arrange the sale for you.

Bedikas Chametz (search for *chametz*): At nightfall on the evening before Pesach, the entire house must be searched to make sure no *chametz* remains, other than that set aside for breakfast and that being sold through a Rabbi. Any other *chametz* found should be set aside for "the burning of *chametz*" in the morning.

Biur Chametz (burning of *chametz*): All *chametz* found during the search from the night before or left over from breakfast must be burned. Consult a reliable authority as to the exact time when eating *chametz* becomes forbidden in the morning and when the remaining *chametz* should be burned.

The proper blessings to be recited for *Bedikas Chametz* and *Biur Chametz* can be found in a Haggadah or *siddur*.

Cleaning Hints

How does one clean a house for Pesach in order to make sure there is no *chametz* in his possession?

On Pesach, not only is the consumption of actual *chametz* food prohibited, but even the smallest particle of *chametz* that makes its way into your kosher-for-Pesach food must not be eaten. Consequently, the home must be cleaned in a way that no *chametz* crumbs remain in areas, clothes or objects that could come into contact with food on Pesach.

Pesach cleaning can be quite complicated. Here are some suggestions:

Start early. Right after Purim is a good idea. There's always more to be done than you expect.

Prevention is always the best timesaver. Keep Pesach in mind all year and train children to eat only in the kitchen and not to travel around the house with food.

Make lists of everything that has to be done in each room, using the guidelines below to make sure you haven't forgotten anything. Pay special attention to the timing of the tasks. Some rooms can be cleaned early. Divide up the tasks into a weekly schedule that you can handle. Differentiate between what is absolutely necessary for Pesach cleaning and what would be nice to do, either for decoration's sake or spring cleaning. List each item in detail and write down how long you think it will take. Break down large tasks, such as a whole closet or dresser to sections and drawers. Don't remove the contents of more shelves than you can complete in a single session.

Wash all curtains. At least two weeks before Pesach, clean the beds and mattresses. A vacuum cleaner is a handy tool for this. At least a week before Pesach, clean the living room thoroughly. Vacuum sofa and chairs, searching for crumbs in crevices. Don't forget to air and dust books, carefully checking the ones used at the table. Rugs and carpets must also be checked for *chametz*.

Medicine Cabinets: These can be cleaned early. Remove all medicines and cosmetics which may contain *chametz*. Lock them away with the other *chametz* you are permitted to sell, such as perfumes and alcoholic beverages. Alternatively, store these medicines and cosmetics in the cabinet after cleaning it and tape or lock it shut. *Kosher l'Pesach* medicines should then be kept in a different place. (Most medicines are available kosher for Pesach, with reliable Rabbinical supervision.) Buy whatever *kosher l'Pesach* medicines you need early. If something you need is not available, consult a Rabbinical authority.

Kitchen and Food Preparations: Take an inventory of foodstuffs, frozen and canned, in your possession that should be used up before Pesach. Two or three weeks before Pesach, thoroughly clean one closet or cupboard. Line it with newspapers or shelving paper. Shop early for matzahs, matzah meal, and all staple Pesach supplies (spices, jams, nuts, etc.). Keep them in this cupboard and add supplies as they are purchased.

Dedicate the last week before Pesach to the kitchen. Clean the freezer and refrigerator first, reserving a section for *chametz* foods that need to be used up before Pesach. Buy meat and fish at least a week before the holiday and freeze them.

During the last week, you can use paper plates to save time. You might give *kosher l'Pesach* cookies to children so they don't spread *chametz* around the house. Make sure they finish eating while still in the kitchen.

All cabinets must be cleaned thoroughly and checked for *chametz*, e.g. crumbs, pieces of grain, etc. Year-round utensils and food items without certification for Pesach, such as spices, as well as *kitniyos* (rice, peas, etc.), must be stored in a locked cabinet during Pesach. Although you are selling the *chametz* in a cabinet, the cabinet itself must be cleaned, checked and locked. For more information on selling *chametz*, see p. 3–4.

Here are some special suggestions for cleaning:

Stove, Oven, Microwave, etc.: A Rabbinical authority should be consulted about how to make the stove and oven *kosher l'Pesach*. Even if you do not plan to use your oven over Pesach, it must be thoroughly cleaned.

Pots, Pans, Utensils, Small Appliances: Items which are not special for Pesach should be cleaned and put away for the duration of the holiday. When cleaning small appliances, a toothbrush is very handy for getting into corners.

Refrigerator: Use baking soda in warm water to give the refrigerator a fresh smell.

Tables and Chairs: Take apart whatever you can without breaking it. Clean underneath, too.

Counters: Scrub thoroughly and cover with contact paper, oil cloth, cardboard, metal, plywood or heavy-duty aluminum foil.

Sinks: Scrub thoroughly with cleanser or bleach. Line with contact paper when dry or use racks and dishpans for washing dishes during the holiday. Discuss this with a Rabbinical authority.

Cupboards and Drawers: Wash out cupboards and drawers several days in advance. Cover shelves with contact paper or shelving paper. Pack away all utensils, appliances, etc., which are not special for Pesach.

Impossible to Clean Places: Bleach and other strong cleaning solutions can be used to render the *chametz* unfit to eat.

What Children Can Do:

Children often enjoy cleaning their own toys. Plastic toys can be thrown into the bathtub for kids to clean. Polishing Pesach silverware is a chore many children enjoy. Children also can be surprisingly helpful in cleaning hard to reach corners.

Children also like to make labels (index card size) on which they write "Closed for Pesach" and attach them to cupboards and closets. They may even enjoy decorating the labels with Pesach symbols.

Two days before Pesach — try to get the house all clean for Pesach. The day before — take out your Pesach utensils and start cooking. Try to get all the cooking done the day before Erev Pesach so that you can rest the day of the Seder. Then sit back and enjoy the Seder with your family and guests.

What Is the Nutritional Content of Matzah vs. Bread?*

Nutritionally, matzah contains one-fourth the water of bread and 30% more calories per equivalent serving. There are roughly equal amounts of protein. On the other hand, matzah has 40% more carbohydrate but 73% less fat than bread. Matzah has only a trace of salt (sodium), with almost no vitamins or minerals. Whole-grain bread, in contrast, has small amounts of the B-vitamins as well as iron and fiber.

In short, matzah is low in salt, low in fat and low in water, and equivalent to bread in its protein content. On the other hand, it is higher in calories and lacks vitamins, minerals and fiber.

We spoke to the nutritionist, Yaakov Levinson, and he recommends drinking lots of water and eating plenty of fresh fruits and vegetables to facilitate digestion.

---

* Taken from *The Jewish Guide to Natural Nutrition*, Yaakov Levinson, Feldheim Publishers.

Erev Pesach

Erev Pesach and the Seder Night

The Seder night is different from all other nights. The Seder experience is indelible, filled with emotion and tradition.

Early in the morning preceding the Seder night, *chametz* becomes forbidden. The last crumbs found during the search the night before are burned and the house is now truly *kosher l'Pesach*. Then everyone joins in preparing for the Seder.

Here are some recipes for the Seder plate:

Z'roa — Shankbone
Roast a fresh chicken wing on the burner until it is browned and tender.

Egg
Hard boil an egg. After boiling, roast it on the burner.

Bitter Herbs
Either use freshly grated horseradish or Romaine lettuce.

Karpas
Boil a potato or use carrot, radish, celery, cucumber or parsley.

Salt Water
Mix and dissolve 1 T. salt in 1/2 cup water.

Charoses for 5 People — Jerusalem Style
5 dates   *a dash of ginger*
1-2 apples   *1/4 tsp. cinnamon*
6 walnuts   *1-3 T. wine*
5 almonds

Grind dates, apples, walnuts and almonds separately. Mix together, adding ginger, cinnamon and enough wine to make it a thick mixture — not to dilute it.

Charoses — Sephardic Style

1/2 lb. (1/4 K.) dates   *1/4 tsp. (100 g.) almonds*
1 apple   *1/8 tsp. pepper*
1/4 lb. (100 g.) walnuts   *1/4 tsp. cinnamon*
wine

Grind all the above together. Add enough wine a few hours before the Seder to make it stick together.

Charoses — Iraqi-Syrian Style

2 lb. (1 K.) dates   *cinnamon*
2 handfuls mixed walnuts and   *wine*
* almonds*

Remove the pits from the dates. Rinse in water. Grind. Cover with water in a pot and cook on a small flame until the mixture becomes dry, stirring occasionally to prevent sticking. This takes about 2 hours. Take out 1 cupful and add ground nuts, a little cinnamon and wine for charoses. The rest of the cooked dates can be used as jam throughout the holiday.

Charoses — American Style

1 cup chopped apples   *1 tsp. cinnamon*
1 cup chopped walnuts   *2 T. sweet wine*

Mix everything together. Add enough wine to bind the mixture.

Suggested Menus

First Seder Night
Seder Plate (pp. 11–12)
Gefilte Fish (p. 46)
Chicken Soup with Kneidlach (pp.17, 24)
Chicken in Wine Sauce (p.33)
Orange Juice Tzimmes (p.76)
Romaine Lettuce Salad (p.78)
Applesauce (p.117)

Second Seder Night
Seder Plate (pp.11–12)
Rich Russian Borsht (p.18)
Chicken Gan Eden (p.35)
Yerushalmi Kugel (p.65)
Arabic Salad (p.74)
Almond Nut Cake with Lemon Filling (p. 93)
Coffee

Holiday Dinner
Gulyas Soup (p.19)
Egg and Onion Appetizer (p.29)
Stuffed Cabbage (p.42)
Beet Salad (p.74)
Grated Potato Kugel (p.65)
Scalloped Eggplant (p.77)
Rhubarb Dessert (p.118)

Friday Night
Israeli Carp (p.49)
Chicken Soup (p.17)
Bubby's Noodles (p.24)
Stuffed Roast Turkey (pp.36, 39)
Matzah-Nut Kugel (p.65)
Tomato Salad (p.80)
Sweet-and-Sour Red Cabbage (p.75)
Chocolate Mousse (p.119)

Shabbat Lunch
Chopped Liver (p.27)
Meat Cholent (p.40)
Assorted Pickles (p.82)
Mashed Potato Kugel (p.66)
Special Beets with Orange Juice (p.74)
Fruit Salad (p.116)
Tea, Black Coffee

Dairy Meal
Potato-Sour Cream Soup (p.22)
Great Eggplant Appetizer (p.28)
Sweet-and-Sour Fish (p.49)
Confetti Vegetables (p.81)
Carrot-Nut Pudding (p.68)
Orange Cake with Lemon Ice (pp.94, 124)
Coffee

Low Fat Dinner
Vegetable Soup (p.19)
Baked Fish with Vegetables (p.48)
Spinach Pie (p.68)
Romaine Lettuce Salad (p.78)
Carrot-Scallion Salad (p.76)
Dill Pickles (p.82)
Baked Apples (p.116)

Soups & Appetizers

SOUPS

Chicken Soup
Chicken Soup with Kneidlach
Rich Russian Borsht
Tomato Borsht
Gazpacho
Quick Onion Soup
Gulyas Soup
Special Cabbage Soup

Vegetable Soup
Cabbage Soup
Pareve Cabbage-Tomato Borsht
Valerie's Potato-Onion Soup
Basic Beet Borsht
Potato Soup
Milchig Borscht
Potato-Sour Cream Soup

SOUP ACCESSORIES

*Egg Drops I
Egg Drops II
Egg Drops III
*Matzah Meal Mandelach
*Pesach Noodles
Bubby's Noodles
*Chow Mein Noodles

Potato Starch Noodles
*Kneidlach
*Mashed Potato Kneidlach
*Grated Potato Kneidach
*Pesach Kneidlach
Kugelach
*Fluffy Kneidlach

APPETIZERS

Chopped Liver
Vegetarian Chopped Liver
Avocado Salad
Avocado-Egg Salad
Broiled Grapefruit
Chopped "Liver" Spread
Stuffed Eggs (Deviled Eggs)
Great Green Pepper Appetizer

Great Eggplant Appetizer
Eggplant Torte
*Baked Stuffed Zucchini
Eggs and Onions Appetizer
Deep Fried Onions
Special Fricassee Appetizer
Letchow I (like Spanish Omelette)
Letchow II

Soups

Chicken Soup

1 chicken, cut into quarters   *1 parsnip*
2–3 medium-sized carrots   *salt, to taste*
1 medium onion   *4 quarts (4 liters) cold water*
several celery stalks

Use large pot (at least 6-quart size). Put in water and bring to a boil. Add chicken and bring to a boil again. Skim. Add vegetables, reduce fire and cook for about 1 1/2 hours until chicken is tender. Remove chicken and vegetables with slotted spoon. Strain soup through fine strainer. Soup can be made Thursday for Shabbat, refrigerated overnight and fat removed before heating for Shabbat meal.

Suggestion: Make a mixture of salt, pepper, garlic and paprika, rub onto chicken pieces and brown in oven to give a roasted taste, if your family doesn't care for soup chicken.

Chicken Soup with Kneidlach

3 chickens   *1 large carrot*
1 large onion   *10–12 cloves garlic*

Clean chickens well in hot water, removing skin and all fat. Cut into serving pieces. Cover chicken and vegetables with water and cook in a pot for 2 hours. Remove from flame and pour off soup, leaving only chicken and vegetables. In a separate pan, fry whole garlic cloves in olive oil until golden brown. Pour over chicken and reheat for 10–15 minutes. Slice cooked carrot and serve on chicken pieces. Reheat soup to boiling, meanwhile preparing kneidlach. (See Soup Accessories.) Makes about 12 servings.

Goes well with mashed potatoes. Mash boiled potatoes. Add remaining garlic sauce to potatoes. This makes a complete meal.

Rich Russian Borsht

8 medium beets
4 onions
1 K. (2 lb.) chuck beef, cut
  into serving portions
1/4 K. (1/2 lb.) soup bones
1/4 medium-size cabbage

3 tomatoes, crushed
Juice of 2 lemons
1 tsp. salt
1 tsp. sugar
10 cups water

Dice and sauté onions. Add shredded beets and cabbage. Simmer until vegetables are soft. Add meat, bones, tomatoes and water. Bring to a boil and simmer until meat is tender. Add lemon juice, salt and sugar to taste. Cook an additional 30 minutes.

Tomato Borsht

4 1/2 lb. (2 K.) tomatoes
1/4 tsp. salt

1 tsp. sugar
1 egg yolk

Cover tomatoes with water in large pot. Cook well until soft. Cool. Mash tomatoes in a colander or strainer with a wooden spoon (if available) until only the peels and seeds are left to be discarded. Add salt and sugar. Beat egg yolk and slowly add 3 T. of the cold borsht. Then add egg-borsht mixture to remaining borsht and mix well.

Gazpacho

3 lb. (1 1/2 K.) ripe tomatoes,
  peeled and cored
2 cups tomato juice or 1 cup
  tomato paste with water
  added to make 2 cups
2 cucumbers, peeled

1/2 cup onion, chopped
1/2 cup green pepper, chopped
3 T. vinegar
fresh garlic
salt and pepper, to taste
1/3 cup olive oil

Chop tomatoes, cucumbers, onion and green peppers finely. Rub bowl with fresh garlic, then add vegetables. Combine tomato juice, olive oil, vinegar, salt and pepper and add to vegetables. Place in refrigerator to chill. Serve cold.

Quick Onion Soup

4 large onions
3 T. oil
2 tsp. potato starch
1/4 tsp. pepper

1 tsp. salt
pareve consomme, diluted
  with water to equal 2 cups

Slice onions in rings and cut in half. Sauté onions in oil. Blend in potato starch. Cook 1 minute, stirring. Add consomme, salt and pepper. Cover and simmer 30 minutes.

Gulyas Soup

1 lb. (1/2 K.) soup meat, cubed
4 T. vinegar
1 clove garlic, crushed
6 cups water
2 potatoes, cubed

3 chopped onions
2 T. oil
1 T. paprika
1 tsp. salt

Marinate meat in vinegar. Fry onions in oil until golden. Add beef and brown lightly. Add water. Add seasonings and simmer for about 2 hours. Add potatoes and cook about 20 minutes.

Special Cabbage Soup

1-2 lb. can (900 g.) peeled
  tomatoes
1 lb. (1/2 K.) cabbage
1 lb. (1/2 K.) flanken
1 apple, cored and quartered

5-6 cups water
soup bones
1 T. sugar
2 T. lemon juice
salt and pepper, to taste

Shred cabbage and cover with 1/2 cup coarse salt. Let stand and squeeze out moisture. Place cabbage, tomatoes, meat, bones and remaining ingredients in soup pot. Cook 2 hours. Taste and adjust seasoning.

Vegetable Soup

3 carrots
2 potatoes
1 bunch of parsley
8 cups water

2 stalks celery
1 onion
2 parsnips
salt and pepper, to taste

Blend all vegetables in blender and cook 30 minutes.

Cabbage Soup

1 lb. (1/2 K.) stew meat
salt and pepper, to taste
diced onion
3 cups water

1 medium cabbage
2 cups tomato juice or 1 cup
tomato paste, adding water
to make 2 cups

Partially cook beef in water with onion and seasonings. Add shredded cabbage with tomato juice. Simmer slowly until cabbage and beef are tender.

Pareve Cabbage-Tomato Borsht

1/2 lb. (250 g.) cabbage
1 lb. (500 g.) tomatoes
5 cups water or broth
1–2 T. lemon juice

1–2 T. sugar or honey
ginger
cloves

Cut cabbage into long, thin strips. Cook until soft in the water or broth. Add all remaining ingredients. Boil until tender. Soup may be served hot or cold.

Valerie's Potato-Onion Soup

8 large onions
6–8 large potatoes

10 cups water
salt and pepper, to taste

Dice onions and fry slowly in a little oil until transparent. Add water, potatoes, seasonings and cook over a low heat until potatoes are soft. Serves 8–10.

Basic Beet Borsht

10 large beets (scrubbed,
peeled and diced)
2 1/2 quarts (2 1/2 liters) water
1 onion, minced

3 tsp. salt
2 T. sugar
1/4 cup lemon juice
2 eggs

Combine first five ingredients in large pot and cook 1 hour. Add lemon juice and season again to taste. Beat 2 eggs in bowl and add hot soup slowly to prevent curdling.
Serving Suggestion: Chill and serve with sour cream or boiled potatoes.

Potato Soup

4 medium potatoes, cubed
small
1 cup celery and carrots,
chopped
1 medium onion, chopped fine

1/2 cup parsley, chopped
1/2 green pepper, chopped fine
pepper and paprika, to taste
1 T. potato starch
1 tsp. oil

Cook chopped carrots and celery for 5 minutes in a pot with about 3 inches of water. In a separate pan, fry onions and add to soup mixture. Next, add potatoes, parsley, green pepper and spices to soup. Brown potato starch in hot oil. Add some of the soup mixture carefully to starch mixture and blend. Add starch mixture to soup and cook until vegetables are tender. Serves about 6.

Milchig Borscht

1 onion, chopped
1 lb. beets, peeled and chopped
1 large apple (cooking)
2 celery stalks, chopped
1/2 red pepper, chopped
4 oz. mushrooms, chopped
2 T. butter
2 T. oil

8 cups stock or water
1 tsp. cumin seed
1 pinch thyme, dried
1 large bay leaf
fresh lemon juice
salt and pepper, to taste
2/3 cup sour cream
sprigs of fresh dill, garnish

Place all chopped vegetables into a large saucepan with the butter, oil and 3 T. of the stock or water. Cover and cook gently for about 15 minutes, shaking the pan occasionally. Stir in the cumin seeds and cook for a minute, then add the remaining stock or water, dried thyme, bay, lemon juice and seasoning. Bring to a boil, cover and gently simmer for 30 minutes. Strain vegetables and reserve liquid. Blend the vegetables in a food processor until smooth and creamy. Return to pan, stir in the reserved stock and reheat. Check seasoning. Serve with swirls of sour cream and a few sprigs of fresh dill.

Potato-Sour Cream Soup

3 large potatoes, cubed   *2–3 carrots, grated*
2 celery stalks, sliced   *salt and pepper, to taste*
2 large onions, diced   *2 cups sour cream*

Wash, clean and cut up vegetables. Place in large pot. Pour 2
1/2–3 cups of boiling water over vegetables. Cover and cook 20
minutes. Add salt and pepper to taste. Add sour cream and stir
until well blended. Continue cooking until vegetables are soft.
Season again to taste.

To reduce fat in soups, refrigerate for several hours or
overnight. Remove and discard congealed fat before reheating.

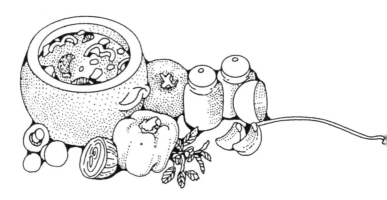

Soup Accessories

*Egg Drops I
2 eggs   *1/4 tsp. salt*
1/2 cup water   *10 T. matzah meal*
Combine well-beaten eggs with salt, water and matzah meal.
Mix thoroughly until mixture is smooth. Drop by spoonfuls
into boiling soup and simmer 2-3 minutes.

Egg Drops II
1/2 egg per portion
Beat eggs. Drop slowly into boiling soup.

Egg Drops III
2 eggs   *salt, to taste*
4 T. potato starch   *8 T. water*
Beat eggs. Add salt. Mix in potato starch and water. Drop
slowly into boiling soup.

*Matzah Meal Mandelach
3 eggs   *1/2 tsp. potato starch*
2/3 cup cake meal   *1/8 tsp. salt*
Beat eggs and add cake meal, potato starch and salt. Knead and
roll out 1/4-inch thick. Cut into 1/4-inch squares. Fry in deep,
hot oil until brown. Remove and drain on absorbent paper.
Serve in hot soup.

*Pesach Noodles
4 eggs   *1 T. matzah cake meal*
4 T. cold water   *1/8 tsp. salt*
Beat all ingredients until well-blended. Heat vegetable oil in
pan. Pour over entire surface in a thin sheet. Fry until set. Turn
out on a kitchen towel. Cool and roll up each sheet. Cut into
thin strips for noodles.

Bubby's Noodles

3 eggs   *1 tsp. salt*
1 tsp. water

Mix all ingredients together. Heat lightly-greased frying pan and pour onto it a thin coat of mixture. Flip out on towel and roll 5 of these egg leaves tightly together. Slice into thin noodles. Serve in hot chicken soup.

*Chow Mein Noodles

1/2 cup matzah meal   *scant 2/3 cup water*
2 T. potato starch

Mix all ingredients together and refrigerate dough for 15 minutes. Remove from refrigerator and divide into 2 balls. Flatten balls of dough on a board covered with some matzah meal. Sprinkle some matzah meal on rolling pin and roll out dough to 1/8-inch thickness. Slice into thin strips or wider strips if desired. Bake on greased cookie sheet at 400° F for 15 minutes until light brown and crispy. Serves 10–12.

Potato Starch Noodles

3 eggs   *1/2 cup potato starch*
1/2 cup water

Beat eggs. Add potato starch and water and beat well. Heat oiled frying pan. Pour into thin sheets and fry both sides. Turn out on paper. Roll up and slice very thin. Add to soup 5 minutes before serving. Can be used to make blintze leaves.

*Kneidlach

3 large or 4 medium eggs   *3/4 cup matzah meal*
1 T. oil   *salt and pepper, to taste*

Beat eggs and oil. Slowly add matzah meal, salt and pepper until you have a thin mixture. Form small balls with wet hands and put them into the boiling soup. They grow a lot in size. Makes 15 kneidlach.

*Mashed Potato Kneidlach

2 cups mashed potatoes	*1 tsp. salt*
2 slightly beaten eggs	*2/3 cup matzah meal*

Add salt and eggs to cooled mashed potatoes and mix well. Add just enough matzah meal to hold mixture together. Form into balls and drop into boiling soup or water. Cook 20 minutes.

*Grated Potato Kneidach

3 large raw potatoes	*1/8 tsp. pepper*
1 1/2 cups matzah meal	*1/2 tsp. salt*
1/4 cup chicken fat	*1/2 cup water*
3 eggs	

Pare and grate potatoes. Squeeze out as much liquid as possible. Combine with rest of ingredients and mix thoroughly. Let stand 1 hour. Form into balls. Drop into boiling salted water or soup. Cook 1 hour.

*Pesach Kneidlach

1 T. congealed fat from top of	*4 eggs*
chicken soup	*1/2 tsp. salt*
1 cup matzah meal	*4 T. chicken soup*

Beat eggs well. Add fat and salt and mix well. Slowly add matzah meal, then chicken soup, blending thoroughly. Refrigerate for at least 1 hour. Boil about 2 1/2 quarts (2 liters) of water in large pot. Shape matzah meal mixture into small balls, wetting hands in between. Drop carefully into boiling water into which 1 tsp. of salt has been added. Cover and boil 1 hour on medium flame. Turn off fire and let stand in pot for 10–15 minutes before removing.

Kugelach

3–4 potatoes	*1/2 tsp. salt*
3 eggs	*oil*

Boil potatoes until tender, but not soft. Mash them. Add the salt and eggs and mix well. Fry the kugelach in oil. Add to soup and cook for 1/2 an hour.

⭑Fluffy Kneidlach

3 eggs, separated   *1/2 tsp. salt*
3/4 cup matzah meal

Beat egg whites until stiff. Add yolks and continue beating. Fold in matzah meal and salt. Let stand 5 minutes. Form into small balls. Drop into boiling soup or water. Cover and simmer 20 minutes.

For variation, add 2 T. chopped liver or 1 cup strained, mashed, cooked vegetables.

Appetizers

Chopped Liver

1/2 lb. (1/4 K.) liver, broiled   *2 medium onions*
4 hard boiled eggs   *salt, to taste*

Dice and fry onions lightly in oil. (Use more onions if you like; they shrink upon frying.) Grind onions, eggs and liver. At end, you can grind through a piece of matzah to clean out all the ingredients. (This will make your chopped liver *gebrokts* .) Mix well. Garnish with grated egg yolk or red pepper strips.

Vegetarian Chopped Liver

4 hard boiled eggs   *salt, to taste*
2 1/2 oz. (75 g.) walnuts   *1 medium onion, chopped*

Grind eggs, walnuts and sautéed onion. Add salt and mix well.

Avocado Salad

1 avocado   *fresh chopped garlic to taste*
milk to soften   *1 onion, chopped*
1/2 green pepper, chopped   *1/2 tomato, chopped*
3 1/2 oz. (100 g.) soft cheese   *salt, to taste*

Mash avocado. Add other ingredients. Mix in milk to soften.

Avocado-Egg Salad

6 lbs. (3 K.) avocados   *lemon juice to taste*
3 hard-boiled eggs   *1/2 tsp. salt*
2 onions, diced

Mash avocado and eggs. Add sautéed onions, lemon juice and salt. Mix well. Best when served immediately.

Broiled Grapefruit

grapefruits   *butter or shortening*
sugar or honey

Cut grapefruits into halves. Loosen each section. Fill center with butter or shortening. Sprinkle with sugar or spread with honey. Broil until browned. Delicious!

Chopped "Liver" Spread

3 T. oil	*1 cup walnuts, chopped*
1/2 lb. (250 g.) mushrooms,	*salt and pepper, to taste*
chopped	*1 T. water*
1 small onion, chopped	

Sauté mushrooms and onion in oil for 8 minutes. Pour into blender or food processor, adding walnuts, seasonings and water. Blend until smooth. Serve as a spread for matzah. Makes about 1 cup.

Stuffed Eggs (Deviled Eggs)

6 eggs	*finely chopped parsley or onion*
mayonnaise	*salt and pepper, to taste*

Hard boil eggs. Put into cold water. Peel carefully and slice in half. Remove yolks and mash, adding a little salt and pepper, finely chopped parsley stems or onion and a little mayonnaise to hold it together. Stuff eggs and top with bits of red or green peppers.

Great Green Pepper Appetizer

4 green peppers	*oil*
2 T. ketchup (or tomato sauce)	*2 T. sugar*
1 small can tomato sauce	*2 large onions*
1 T. lemon juice	*1/2 tsp. mayonnaise*

Boil peppers. Peel and slice into strips. Sauté onions. Add tomato sauce, ketchup, lemon juice, sugar and pepper. Cook in sauce 15 minutes. Cool. Add mayonnaise. Serve cold.

Great Eggplant Appetizer

1 large eggplant, peeled and	*1 small onion, chopped*
diced	*mayonnaise*
1 sour pickle, diced	*salt, to taste*
1/2 green pepper, diced	

Simmer eggplant in a little water on a small flame until tender. Drain, cool and mash. Add other ingredients and mix. Refrigerate.

Eggplant Torte

Make dough for Potato Starch Noodles (see Soup Accessories).
Fry 6–8 blintz leaves. Layer alternately with this filling:

1 lb. (1/2 K.) eggplant	*2 eggs*
4 T. oil	*3 onions*
2 cloves fresh garlic, chopped	*salt and pepper, to taste*

Peel eggplant. Pour over boiling water to cover and leave for 30
minutes. Dice onions and steam in oil. Chop eggplant and
steam with onions for 30 minutes. Add chopped, fresh garlic,
salt, pepper, 2 eggs. Stir. Cook a few more minutes. Put
between blintze leaves. Top with tomato sauce.
Variation: Add leftover cooked, diced meat or chicken to
eggplant.

*Baked Stuffed Zucchini

2 zucchini, cut in half	*1/2 tsp. parsley*
lengthwise	*1 clove garlic, chopped*
1 small onion, finely chopped	*2 T. matzah meal*
4 T. tomato sauce	

Scoop pulp out of zucchini halves. Cook pulp, onion, sauce and
spices in a pan for 5 minutes. Add matzah meal and mix well.
Restuff zucchini with mixture. Place in a baking dish with a
little water on bottom. Bake at 450° F (225 °C) for 30 minutes
until zucchini shells are soft.

Eggs and Onions Appetizer

6 hard boiled eggs	*3/4 tsp. salt*
1/2 cup chopped onions	*1/4 tsp. white pepper*
2 T. congealed chicken fat	

Chop all ingredients together and serve on lettuce leaves. Top
with tomato slices.

Deep Fried Onions

Cut onions into rings. Dip into noodle dough mixture (see Soup
Accessories). Season with salt and pepper. Drop by spoonfuls
into deep hot oil. Fry until brown.

Special Fricassee Appetizer

2 T. oil
chicken parts, raw or cooked
1 lb. (1/2 K.) onion, sliced
4 large carrots, shredded
salt and pepper, to taste

1 cup mashed potatoes or 1/2
  cup potato starch mixed
  with a little water
chopped fresh garlic
chopped parsley

Heat oil. Add chicken parts, onions and carrots. Steam until tender. Add mashed potatoes or potato starch mixture. Stir and season with salt, pepper, garlic and parsley.

Letchow I *(like Spanish Omelette)*

2 tomatoes, sliced
2 peppers, diced
2 onions, diced
pepper, to taste

3 T. oil
6 eggs
1 tsp. salt

Fry vegetables slowly in oil for about 15 minutes, until soft. Drop in eggs. Sprinkle with salt and pepper. Scramble until set.

Letchow II

2 tomatoes, diced
5 zucchini squash, diced
2 onions, diced
1 carrot, diced

6 eggs
2/3 cup cooked chicken, diced
5 T. oil
salt and pepper, to taste

Prepare same as for Letchow I.

And, on to the Meal

POULTRY

Chicken Cholent without Beans
Oriental Chicken
*Chicken in Wine Sauce
Gourmet Roasted Chicken
  on Potato Straw Mats
Chicken Paprikash
Chicken Cacciatore
Chicken Gan Eden
Dieter's "Fried" Chicken

*Fricassee
*Chicken and Potato Patties
*Turkey Shnitzel
Roast Turkey
Chicken Hash
*Chicken Pot Pie
Fried Turkey Cakes
Shnitzel Roll-Ups

STUFFINGS

*Matzah Stuffing
*Mushroom and Onion Stuffing

*Potato Stuffing

MEAT

Meat Cholent
Cholent
Hamburgers
Hamburger Omelette Foo Yong
*Homemade Sausages for Pesach
Meat Loaf
Economical Beef Casserole
Sautéed Liver
*Sweet-and-Sour Meatballs
*Stuffed Cabbage

Roast Tongue
Meat Tzimmes with
  Potato Dumplings
*Potato Dumplings
Meat with Okra
Stuffed Peppers over Cabbage
Baked Beef Stew
Roast Beef
Roast in the Wonder Pot
Leftover Roast

FISH

*Gefilte Fish
*Mock Gefilte Fish
Fish Loaf
Not Gebrokts Gefilte Fish
*Fluffy Gefilte Fish
*Baked Fish Rolls
Fish-Stuffed Potato Boats

Baked Fish with Vegetables
Israeli Carp
Sweet-and-Sour Fish
Fish in Cream
*Fish Patties
Fisherman's Stew

Poultry

Chicken Cholent without Beans

1 chicken
1–2 lb. (1/2–1 K.) french fried
  potatoes

1 1/2 cups water (at least)
salt, pepper and garlic, to taste
cinnamon and sugar, to taste

Sprinkle chicken with salt and pepper. Rub with garlic. Roast covered with 1/2 cup water for 1 1/2 hours, uncovering for last 30 minutes. Cut into serving pieces. Bake or fry french fries, seasoning with cinnamon and sugar. Add to chicken with 1 1/2 cups of water (at least) and put on Shabbos hot plate until next day.

Oriental Chicken

1 cut-up chicken
1/2 cup honey
1 can crushed pineapple

8 T. oil
1/4 cup lemon juice

Wash and drain chicken pieces. Put 4 T. oil in baking dish. Roll pieces in oil to coat. Put 4 T. oil in saucepan. Place chicken pieces skin down, and bake at 350° F (175° C) for 30 minutes. Stir in honey, lemon juice and pineapple until mixed thoroughly. Turn chicken. Bake, basting several times with syrup and gravy until tender and glazed.

*Chicken in Wine Sauce

1 chicken, cut into serving
  pieces
1 cup potato starch or matzah
  meal

2 onions, diced
1 cup wine
mushrooms (optional)
salt and pepper, to taste

Sauté onions (mushrooms optional). "Bread" chicken (put chicken pieces into plastic bag with matzah meal or potato starch, salt and pepper to taste and shake so they become coated). Fry in onions and mushrooms until brown. Put in pan filled with boiling water to cover chicken. Include in water 1 cup wine. Cook on top of stove on very low flame for about 2 hours.

Gourmet Roasted Chicken on Potato Straw Mats

1 chicken	2 T. margarine
1 lb. (500 g.) potatoes, coarsely grated	salt and pepper, to taste

Preheat the oven to 400° F. Place chicken in a small roasting pan, breast side up. Roast 1 1/4 hours. Plunge grated potatoes into cold water. Drain. Plunge and rinse once more. Pat very dry. Melt 1 tsp. margarine in a 6-inch wide nonstick skillet. When the margarine is hot, swirl it around the bottom, add 1 cup grated potatoes and smooth down the surface. Sprinkle with salt and pepper and place 2 tsp. of margarine around the sides of the potato mat. Cover the skillet and cook on medium flame for 10 minutes. Lift the lid twice during that time, lifting it straight up so the steam won't fall back into the potatoes, and dry the underside of the lid. Cover again. After 10 minutes, check the mat's underside. When it's crisp and golden, invert the potato mat onto a plate. Add a bit more margarine to the skillet and when it sizzles, slide the potato mat back into the pan. Cook uncovered for about 5 minutes or until the underside is crisp and golden. Repeat with the next 3 potato mats. (If you make larger mats — in a 10-inch skillet — use 2 cups of grated potatoes and cook 15–20 minutes on the first side and about 10 minutes on the second side.) Use the chicken juices for gravy. Serve roasted chicken on individual potato straw mats. Pour gravy over them. Decorate with greens.

Chicken Paprikash

1-3 lb. (1 1/4 K.) chicken	salt and pepper, to taste
2 large onions, minced	1 tomato, cut into eighths
1 green pepper, minced	2 T. cooking fat
2 stalks celery, diced	1 tsp. paprika

Season chicken with salt and pepper. Fry onions in fat and add vegetables, chicken and tomatoes. Add a little water to make more gravy. Keep on low flame to prevent burning. Cook until tender.

Chicken Cacciatore

2 small chickens
2 cups tomato sauce
1 minced garlic clove
1/4 tsp. pepper
1 medium-sized onion (1/2
  cup, chopped)

1 large green pepper, seeded
  and sliced
2 cups water
1/2 cup wine
1/2 tsp. salt

Simmer chicken in water for 30 minutes. Remove and cool until easy to handle. Refrigerate 2 cups of stock. Remove meat from chicken and discard skin and bones. Skim fat from stock and put chicken, stock and remaining ingredients into a saucepan, cover and simmer 20 minutes. Uncover and simmer 10 minutes more until sauce has thickened.

Chicken Gan Eden

1 chicken
1/4 tsp. ginger
2 T. honey
2 oranges, cut into sections

2 T. potato starch (optional)
1/4 cup oil
1/4 tsp. cinnamon
1 cup orange juice

Cut up chicken into serving pieces. Brown pieces in oil. Remove chicken. Put potato starch, spices and honey into pan. Mix. Add orange juice and chicken. Cover and simmer until tender. Add orange sections. Reheat and serve.

Dieter's "Fried" Chicken

This chicken cooks golden brown with no fat and no turning.

1 2 lb. (1 K.) chicken,
  cut into quarters
1 tsp. salt

2 large onions, sliced
1/8 tsp. pepper
1/2 cup water

Place skinned chicken sections in a single layer in a large frying pan. Sprinkle with salt and pepper, place onions on top. Cover tightly. Cook over low heat 30 minutes. Tilt lid slightly so liquid will evaporate; continue cooking 20 minutes longer or until chicken is tender and golden. Remove chicken onto heated serving platter. Put onions back into pan, stir in water and browned bits from pan. Cook until liquid evaporates. Spoon over chicken.

*Fricassee

chicken giblets	3 medium onions, diced
2 lb. (1 K.) ground beef	2 eggs
2 broken-up matzahs	2 tsp. salt
2/3 cup cold water	1/4 tsp. pepper
2 tsp. paprika	

Cut giblets into small pieces. Add onions. Cover with water and simmer until tender, approximately 1 1/2 hours. Soak matzahs in water and combine with beef and beaten eggs. Shape into meat balls and drop into hot giblet mixture. Add seasonings, cover and simmer for another 30 minutes.

*Chicken and Potato Patties

1 diced onion	2 T. fat
2 cups cooked chicken, ground	salt and pepper, to taste
2 eggs	1/2 cup matzah meal
2 cups mashed potatoes	

Mix all ingredients together. Form into patties and fry in chicken fat.

*Turkey Shnitzel

4 large slices turkey breast	matzah meal, as needed
salt, pepper and paprika, to taste	2 eggs

Coat each turkey slice with egg. Mix dry ingredients and coat turkey slices in mixture. Fry in deep oil until golden on both sides. Drain thoroughly and serve with lemon wedges or Wine Sauce (see Frostings and Sauces).

Roast Turkey

Clean a medium-sized turkey. Place turkey in a shallow roasting pan. Prick skin all over with a fork so that fat runs out freely. Sprinkle with salt, pepper and paprika to taste. If desired, pack into cavity 2-3 large peeled, cored and quartered cooking apples or other stuffing (see Stuffings). Roast in moderately hot oven, 375° F (190° C). Serve with gravy. Allow 25 minutes per 1b. (400 g.) for roasting time.

Chicken Hash

1 1/2 lb. (600 g.) cooked
   chicken, diced
4 medium potatoes, boiled and
   diced
2 medium green peppers,
   chopped

1 cup celery, cooked and diced
2 cups chicken broth
2 medium tomatoes, sliced
1 T. onion, diced
1/2 cup tomato sauce

Combine chicken, potatoes, peppers and celery in chopping
bowl and chop finely. Add onion, broth and tomato sauce. Place
in casserole dish and top with tomato slices. Bake at 350° F
(175° C) for 30 minutes. Serves 4.

*Chicken Pot Pie

2 cups cooked chicken, ground
1 diced onion
2 eggs
2 cups mashed potatoes

2 T. fat
salt and pepper, to taste
1/2 cup matzah meal

Combine meat, vegetables (reserving 1 cup mashed potatoes for
topping), seasonings, and mix well. Place in greased casserole
dish. Cover with gravy and top with mashed potatoes. Bake for
30 minutes at 350° F (175° C).
Variation: Can be made with chicken or meat pieces, too, each
approximately 1/2-inch square.

Fried Turkey Cakes

1/2 lb. (1/4 K.) turkey, minced
1 lb. (1/2 K.) potatoes, mashed
1 small onion, grated
2 eggs

salt and pepper, to taste
1 tsp. parsley, diced
potato starch
oil

Combine the minced turkey with the mashed potatoes. Add the
grated onion, diced parsley, salt and pepper to taste. Bind with a
little beaten egg. Shape into 8 cakes, coat lightly with potato
starch, then dip in beaten egg. Fry in oil until brown or bake 30
minutes on a greased baking sheet.
Variation: Dip in tomato sauce or ketchup and bake 30 minutes.

Shnitzel Roll-Ups

4 pieces turkey or chicken
shnitzel
3 T. oil

1/4 cup white wine
3/4 cup beef or chicken soup

Filling I:

green peppers, onions and tomatoes

Filling II:

almonds and onions

Filling III:

eggplant, tomatoes and onions

Sauté cut-up filling in oil. Spread on shnitzel slices, roll up and secure with toothpicks. Place around bottom of a wonder pot. Add soup and wine. Bake 1 hour.

Stuffings

*Matzah Stuffing

1 cup hot chicken soup
2 onions, diced
3 eggs, beaten
6 mushrooms, sliced
1/4 cup shmaltz or oil

9 matzahs, crumbled
2 celery stalks, diced
1/2 green pepper, diced
2 tsp. salt

Pour hot soup over matzahs and let stand until absorbed.
Brown onions, celery, mushrooms and peppers. Combine both
mixtures and mix thoroughly with eggs.
Enough for a 5–6 lb. (2–3 K.) chicken.

*Mushroom and Onion Stuffing

1 oz. (25 g.) butter or shortening
1/4 lb. (100 g.) mushrooms,
sliced
1 tsp. parsley, finely chopped

1 small onion, grated
1/4 cup matzah meal
salt and pepper, to taste
2 tsp. olive oil
1/4 cup potato starch

Heat shortening in pan. Add mushrooms and onions and fry 5
minutes. Stir in matzah meal, potato starch, oil, parsley, salt
and pepper. Bind with egg, if necessary. Fill cavity of bird with
stuffing or roll up fish with layer of stuffing.

*Potato Stuffing

2 cups hot mashed potatoes
3/4 cup matzah meal
1 small onion, chopped

1 tsp. parsley, chopped
3 T. oil
1 egg

Combine all ingredients and season well. Add liquid, if
necessary.

Meat

Meat Cholent

4 lb. (2 K.) chuck steak
salt, pepper and paprika, to
   taste

2 large onions, diced
10 potatoes
1 T. honey

Brown meat and onions in a large Dutch oven. Add remaining
ingredients and 1 cup water. Simmer on a low flame about 1
1/2 hours (before Shabbos). Add boiling water. Cook for 20
minutes in tightly covered pot. Place on Shabbos hot plate until
next day's lunch.

Variation: Before cooking for last 20 minutes, add matzah
balls (see Kneidlach in Soup Accessories).

Cholent

1 lb. (1/2 K.) beef
3-4 soup bones
4-5 potatoes

1 medium onion
2 T. oil
2 tsp. fried onions

Put onion, bones, peeled potatoes, fried onions and oil into a
pot. Place meat on top of these ingredients. Fill the pot with
water and place on the fire. Simmer 1 hour before putting on
Shabbos hot plate.

Variation: Add matzah balls (see Kneidlach in Soup
Accessories) 30 minutes before putting it on the Shabbos hot
plate.

Hamburgers

1 1/2 lb. (600 g.) ground beef
4 T. onion, grated
2 cloves garlic, minced
2 tsp. salt
3 T. fat

2 onions, diced
1/4 cup potatoes, grated
1 egg
1/4 cup water
1/4 tsp. pepper

Mix the beef, grated onion, garlic, salt, pepper, potato, egg and
water together. Form into hamburgers. Melt the fat in a pan
and brown the burgers and diced onions for 15 minutes,
turning them after 10 minutes.

Hamburger Omelette Foo Yong

3/4 cup ground beef
1/3 cup onions, finely chopped
6 eggs, separated
2 T. parsley, diced

1 1/4 tsp. salt
1/4 tsp. pepper
2 T. shortening

Beat egg yolks until thick and lemon colored. Blend in raw beef, onion, parsley, salt and pepper. Fold in stiffly-beaten egg whites. In frying pan, melt shortening. Using 1/3 cup mixture for each omelette, cook over medium heat 3 minutes on each side. Add more shortening, if necessary. Makes 6 servings.

*Homemade Sausages for Pesach

1 lb. (1/2 K.) ground beef
1 onion, grated
1 small carrot
fine matzah meal

1 egg
2 T. cold water
salt, to taste

Combine all ingredients, except matzah meal. Roll sausages 1/2 inch thick by 2 1/2 inches long. Roll in matzah meal and fry until brown on all sides.

Meat Loaf

2 lb. (1 K.) ground meat
1 cup tomato juice
1 onion, finely chopped
2 cups potatoes, shredded

1 tsp. salt
1 carrot, shredded
1 T. parsley, chopped
2 eggs, slightly beaten

Preheat oven to 375° F (190° C). Mix all ingredients together and place into greased loaf pan. Bake one hour or until done.

Economical Beef Casserole

2 lb. (1 K.) ground meat
dash pepper
1 green pepper, diced
1 eggplant, peeled and cut into
  small pieces

1/2 tsp. salt
1 cup tomato juice
1 small onion, minced

Mix all ingredients thoroughly. Pour into large pan and bake 45 minutes at 350° F (175° C).

Sautéed Liver

4 very large onions
salt, pepper and paprika, to
   taste

fresh mushrooms
1 lb. (1/2 K.) liver, kashered
   within 3 days of slaughtering

Sauté onions and mushrooms in a little oil. Season with salt, pepper and a lot of paprika. Keep on low fire for about 1 hour, stirring frequently. Add broiled, cubed liver and simmer 10 minutes more. *Kashrus note:* The only type of liver that can be used in this recipe is liver that was kashered within 3 days of slaughtering. You cannot use liver that was frozen for more than 3 days before kashering, even if you broil it first now.

*Sweet-and-Sour Meatballs

1 lb. (1/2 K.) ground beef
1 onion, chopped
1/2 tsp. pepper
juice of 1 lemon

1 egg
1 tsp. salt
2 T. matzah meal
1/2 cup sugar

Mix meat, onion, egg, salt and pepper. Stir in matzah meal. Form into 1-inch balls. Fill large pot half full with water, add lemon juice and sugar. When water is boiling, add meatballs and simmer for about 3 hours. Can even leave meatballs on Shabbos hot plate all night. Add water, if necessary.

*Stuffed Cabbage

15 large cabbage leaves
1 lb. (1/2 K.) ground beef
1 matzah, broken
1/2 cup water
1 egg, beaten

1 large onion, diced
1/4 cup lemon juice
1/2 cup sugar
1/4 cup water
1 can tomato sauce

Place leaves in a large pot and cover with boiling water for 5 minutes. Drain. Soak broken matzah in the 1/2 cup water until soft. Combine this mixture with ground meat and egg. Place a heaping tablespoon of mixture in the center of each leaf. Fold in the sides to cover meat and roll up. Place rolls with open sides down into a large saucepan. Combine remaining ingredients and pour over cabbage rolls. Bring to a boil and then reduce heat. Simmer about 1 1/2 hours.

Roast Tongue

4 1/2 lb. (2 K.) beef tongue
salt water
fresh garlic (optional)
3 onions, sliced
3 whole carrots

1/2 tsp. pepper
1/2 tsp. paprika
3 T. oil
1 cup water or wine

Boil tongue 2 hours in salted water to cover. Peel and place in
roasting pan. Sprinkle with seasonings. Brown onions in hot fat
and put all around tongue. Add carrots and liquid and cover
tightly. Roast 1 additional hour, basting occasionally. Slice only
when cool.

Meat Tzimmes with Potato Dumplings

3-4 lb. (1 1/2 K.) brisket
2 medium onions, chopped
2 T. potato starch

salt and pepper, to taste
3 cups boiling water

Wipe the brisket dry and rub in 2 tsp. salt and 1/2 tsp. pepper.
Brown meat in a large Dutch oven over low heat with chopped
onions. Remove and stir potato starch into meat drippings.
Gradually add 3 cups boiling water. Add 1 tsp. salt. Bring to a
boil and stir. Simmer covered 1 hour. Preheat oven to 375° F
(190° C) and add:

8 carrots, quartered
3 sweet potatoes, quartered

1/4 cup honey
1 cup prunes, pitted

Bake covered for 2 hours or until meat is tender. Remove cover
for last 15 minutes.

Variation: Add Potato Dumpling (see recipe below) before last
hour of cooking.

★ Potato Dumplings

4 large potatoes
2 T. margarine, or other fat or
   oil
1/3 cup matzah meal

1 T. minced onions
2 eggs
1/2 tsp. salt
1 dash pepper

Cook 1 of the potatoes. Grate the other 3 and press out the
liquid. Combine all. Shape into 2 dumplings. Put in center of
tzimmes and cook.

Meat with Okra

1 lb. (1/2 K.) beef
1 lb. (1/2 K.) tomatoes, peeled
  and diced
1 lb. (1/2 K.) okra
1 onion, diced

salt and pepper, to taste
oil
1 cup water
juice of 1/2 lemon

Sauté meat in oil in skillet. Add onions and continue cooking for 5 minutes. Add tomatoes and 1/2 cup water. Arrange okra on top of meat in rows. Add salt, pepper, lemon juice and 1/2 cup water. Cover and cook 45 minutes.

Stuffed Peppers over Cabbage

4 medium green peppers
1 cup leeks, sliced lengthwise
2 lb. (1 K.) ground beef
1/4 cup tomato sauce

4 cups cabbage, shredded
salt and pepper, to taste
1 cup carrots, sliced

Brown the beef in a frying pan. Transfer to a bowl. Season with salt and pepper and moisten with the tomato sauce. Mix. Pack the mixture into the peppers. Put cabbage into the bottom of a pot. Add a layer of leeks and a layer of carrots. Place stuffed peppers on top and pour in enough boiling water to cover cabbage. Sprinkle lightly with salt, cover pot tightly and simmer 45 minutes to 1 hour. 4 servings. This can be a meal in itself.

Baked Beef Stew

1 lb. (1/2 K.) stew meat, cubed
1/2 onion, chopped
1 T. potato starch
2 cups cooked tomatoes
3/4 cup carrots

1/2 cup potato, diced
1 T. oil
2 cloves garlic
salt, to taste
1/2 cup celery

Brown meat in oil. Add onion, salt, carrots, celery, potatoes, garlic, tomatoes and water to cover. Bring to boiling point. Thicken with potato starch stirred into a little water first. Pour evenly into wonder pot and bake 1 1/2 to 2 hours.

Roast Beef

5 lb. (2 1/2 K.) roast   *juice of one orange*
2 large onions   *2 T. wine*
2 green peppers   *fresh garlic*
2 stalks celery

Put roast in heavy foil. Cover with sliced onions, peppers, celery and orange juice. Rub with fresh garlic, if desired. Pour wine over meat. Wrap foil tightly. Roast at 350° F (175° C) for 2 1/2 hours.

Roast in the Wonder Pot

1 1/2 lb. (750 g.) roasting meat   *1 medium onion, sliced*
3 T. oil   *several carrots, sliced*
1 T. red wine   *soup mix*
salt and pepper, to taste

Put oil in wonder pot. Add onion. Place meat in wonder pot and sear on all sides. Add carrots, salt and pepper. Sprinkle with soup powder and water. Roast about 50 minutes, basting once or twice. Add wine and cook a few minutes longer.

Leftover Roast

2 onions, chopped   *meat, cut into pieces*
1 carrot, sliced thin   *red wine*
1/2 eggplant, diced   *oil*
1/2 cup water   *salt and pepper, to taste*
spices, to taste

In a large skillet, sauté onions in oil until brown. Sear meat and add all other ingredients, adding the wine last. Simmer covered for 30 minutes.

Fish

★ Gefilte Fish

4 lb. (2 K.) carp, skinned and boned	1 carrot
6 eggs	2–3 T. matzah meal
6 medium onions	salt and pepper, to taste
	sugar

Grind fish. Fry, grind and strain 5 onions. Add matzah meal, eggs, 1 tsp. salt, 1/4 tsp. pepper and 1/2 tsp. sugar to make a thick mixture. Prepare a large pot 1/4 filled with water. Add fish bones, carrot, onions, a little salt, pepper and sugar. When the water boils, make fish balls from fish mixture and drop them in. Cook on a medium flame 1 1/2–2 hours. Makes 15 servings.

★ Mock Gefilte Fish

1 can tuna fish	2 eggs
4 T. matzah meal	salt and pepper, to taste
1 onion, diced	2–3 carrots, sliced
1 onion, grated	3 cups water

Place diced onions, carrots, salt and pepper with a little water in pot. Boil 2 minutes. Drain tuna and mash well. Add grated onion, eggs, and mix until smooth. Add matzah meal and mix. Form balls and place in boiling water. Make only one layer of balls at a time and cook approximately 30 minutes.

Fish Loaf

2 lb. (1 K.) ground fish	1/4 tsp. pepper
1 carrot	1 tsp. salt
1 medium onion	3 eggs
2 stalks celery	1 T. oil
2 T. nuts, ground	pinch of garlic powder
1 cup tomato sauce	1/3 tsp. paprika

Mix ground fish, carrot, onion and celery. Mix in rest of ingredients, except tomato paste. Bake in well-greased pan for 45 minutes at 350° F (175° C). Pour tomato sauce on fish loaf. Bake 15 minutes more.

Not Gebrokts Gefilte Fish

2 lb. (1 K.) Kassif (or white-
    fish)
1 lb. (1/2 K.) Jaffa fish (or pike)
1 lb. (1/2 K.) onions

4 hard-boiled eggs
salt, sugar and pepper, to taste
1 carrot
4 eggs

Fry onion in covered pot on a small flame in a little oil. Drain well. Grind the onions. Drain well again. Grind the 2 types of fish and the 4 hard-boiled eggs together. Add ground onions and the rest of the ingredients to the fish. Mix very well before cooking until the mixture is dough-like. Prepare a large pot, 1/4 filled with water, with an onion, a carrot, the bones, head, salt, pepper and sugar. When water is boiling, add balls or patties of fish. Cook for at least 1 1/2 hours on medium flame.

⋆ Fluffy Gefilte Fish

4 lb. (2 K.) mixture of filleted
    carp or mixed carp and
    burre or sole
4 medium onions
1/3 cup matzah meal
3 carrots, sliced

3 eggs
1 tsp. pepper
4 tsp. salt
2 T. sugar
1/2– 3/4 cup cold water

If starting with whole carp, cut into inch slices, removing most of the flesh and leaving bone in center. Grind fish with 2 onions. Add salt, sugar and pepper to taste. Add 3 eggs and matzah meal and mix well, also adding cold water. Blend fish mixture thoroughly so water is absorbed into mixture. This insures soft fish balls. Place head of fish in pot with sliced carrots, two sliced onions, salt and pepper. Add 4 cups of water. Bring to boil and cook about 20 minutes. Fill fish skins with mixture and make balls of rest. Cover and simmer for 1 1/2 to 2 hours. Taste stock for additional seasoning, if necessary. Cool fish for 30 minutes. Remove to a platter and garnish with carrot slices. Stock may be strained and put into refrigerator to jell, then cut into pieces to serve with fish.

* Baked Fish Rolls

8 flounder fillets   8 tomato slices
2 eggs   1 cup spinach
8 T. matzah meal   salt and pepper, to taste

Cook spinach, drain and chop. Mix together with beaten eggs, matzah meal and seasonings. Divide mixture on fillets and roll up each one. Fasten with toothpicks. Place fillets on well-greased dish and place a slice of tomato on top of each. Dot with butter and bake in moderate oven 325° F (165° C) about 30 minutes. For variation, fresh mushrooms and sautéed onions may replace spinach.

Fish-Stuffed Potato Boats

4 potatoes   4 T. hot milk
1 lb. (1/2 K.) fish, cooked   1 tsp. onion, grated
paprika, to taste

Bake scrubbed potatoes at 425°F (210° C) for 40-50 minutes. When soft, cut in half lengthwise. Remove insides, leaving skin intact. Mash insides of potatoes together with fish, hot milk and onion. Divide mixture equally into 8 potato halves, piling high in center. Sprinkle paprika on top. Set aside until ready to use, then bake in shallow pan at 400° (200° C) until hot and brown on top.

Baked Fish with Vegetables

3 potatoes, sliced   3 carrots, sliced
3 onions, sliced   1 garlic clove, crushed
1/2 cup celery, sliced   1 T. salt
3 summer squash, sliced   pepper, to taste
1 3-lb. (1 1/4 K.) fish, cut into oil (optional)
  portion-sized pieces   1/4 cup water
3 tomatoes, sliced

Make layers of potatoes, carrots, onions, garlic, celery and squash in wonder pot. Place fish pieces on top. Cover with tomatoes, salt, pepper, and oil if desired. Bake 30 minutes, then add water and bake 30 minutes more.

Israeli Carp

1 lb. (1/2 K.) carp, whole   pepper
1 carrot   2 T. sugar
1 onion

Clean out insides of fish. Cut fish into 4 or 5 slices. Put fish slices into pot with other ingredients and water to cover. Simmer 1–1 1/2 hours. Cool. When cold, remove fish into bowl or onto platter, cutting carrot into slices for decoration. Strain broth and pour over fish or put broth into a separate bowl. Refrigerate to jell.

Sweet-and-Sour Fish

6 slices salmon or carp   2 onions, sliced thin
1 cup sugar   2 lemons, sliced
2 cups water   2 tsp. salt
1 cup vinegar (or lemon juice)   1/2 tsp. ginger

Combine all ingredients except fish and bring to a boil. Add fish, cover and cook over low flame until fish is flaky (about 15 minutes). Cool and refrigerate at least 2 days before serving. Lasts up to 2 weeks refrigerated.

Fish in Cream

4–5 sprigs parsley   1/4 tsp. onion, grated
1 lemon, sliced   salt, pepper and paprika, to
fish fillets   taste
1 cup sour cream

Lay parsley in baking dish and add lemon slices. Place fish on top. Sprinkle with salt and pepper. Bake at 400° F (200° C) until tender. Mix cream and onion and spread over fish. Sprinkle with paprika. Broil until cream is slightly brown and bubbly. Serve hot.

* Fish Patties

1 lb. (1/2 K.) fish fillets
1 medium onion, minced
3 medium potatoes
1 tsp. parsley
salt and pepper, to taste
matzah meal, as needed

Boil all ingredients until potatoes are soft and fish can be flaked. Drain water and mash all together. Form into patties. Add matzah meal for dough-like consistency, if needed. Fry in oil until well-browned.

Fisherman's Stew

1 lb. (400 g.) frozen fish fillets
3 T. butter
3 cups potatoes, sliced
1 1/3 cups cooked tomatoes
1 small onion, chopped
1/4 cup green pepper, chopped
1/4 tsp. pepper
1 tsp. salt

Cook potatoes in butter until brown. Add tomatoes, onion, green pepper and water to cover. Cover and cook 15–20 minutes. Cut fish into 1-inch chunks and add to vegetables with salt and pepper. Cook 10–15 minutes longer.

Dairy Dishes

*Matzah Brei
*Dry Matzah Brei
*Granola
*Cheese Pancakes
*Cheese Blintzes
*Fried Cheese Balls
*Matzah-Cheese Kugel
*Pesach "Lasagne"
*Matzahs and Cheese
Fried Eggs with Special Sauce
Egyptian Omelette
Spanish Omelette
*Cheese-Stuffed Tomatoes
Potato-Cheese Dish

Spicy Eggplant Special
*Pesach Spinach Square
Farmer's Chop Suey
*Passover Pizza
*Eggplant Casserole
*Creamy Potatoes
Pepper Potatoes
Delicious Potato-Egg Casserole
Vegetable-Cheese Spread
Potato-Cheese Kugel
Zucchini Casserole
*Spinach-Cheese Kugel
Spinach Souffle
*Leek, Potato & Matzah Gratin

*Matzah Brei

3 matzahs	2 eggs
1/2 cup milk	1 tsp. salt
1 T. butter	

Soak matzahs in water and drain. Mix with beaten eggs, milk and salt. Fry on both sides until brown. Serve as main dish, or as dessert with cooked fruit, or sprinkled with sugar and cinnamon.

*Dry Matzah Brei

2 eggs, beaten	2 1/2 matzahs
1 tsp. salt	

Break matzahs into small pieces. Dip in beaten egg and salt mixture. Fry in a little oil.

*Granola

3 cups matzah farfel	1/3 cup sugar or honey
1 cup shredded coconut	1/2 cup raisins
1 cup chopped nuts	cinnamon, salt, and grated
1/4 cup oil	orange rind, to taste

Combine farfel, coconut and nuts. Spread onto lightly oiled cookie sheet. Bake 20 minutes at 350° F (175° C), tossing several times. Meanwhile, in a 2-quart saucepan, combine oil, sugar or honey and salt. Simmer, stirring constantly. Add farfel-coconut-nut mixture. Stir until pieces are coated evenly. Add desired seasoning. Spread on cookie sheet. Bake 20 minutes at 350° F (175° C), turning over frequently until brown. Remove and cool. Add raisins. Break up any large chunks with a spatula. Store in closed container in the refrigerator.

*Cheese Pancakes

1/2 lb. (250 g.) cottage cheese	1/2 tsp. salt
4 eggs, well beaten	1 T. sugar
1 tsp. butter, melted	1/2 cup matzah meal

Mix well and fry in hot fat. Serve sprinkled with powdered sugar or jam.

*Cheese Blintzes

3 eggs	*1/2 tsp. salt*
3/4 cup matzah cake flour	*1/2 cup water*

Beat eggs. Add salt, flour and water to make a thin batter. Put 3 T. of batter in a hot greased pan, spreading out as thin as possible. Fry brown on one side. Turn out on a towel. Cool and spread with filling. Fold sides in and roll up. Fry again lightly, turning once to brown both sides. Serve with sour cream.

Filling:

Mix together:

1/2 lb. (250 g.) cottage cheese	*1/2 tsp. salt*
1 egg	*1 T. sour cream*
1/2 tsp. sugar	

*Fried Cheese Balls

1 lb. (1/2 K.) soft cheese	*1 tsp. onion, grated*
3–4 T. matzah meal	*salt and pepper, to taste*
chopped almonds	

Mix together all ingredients, except almonds. Make walnut-sized balls from the mixture and roll in the chopped almonds. Chill the balls in the refrigerator for about 1 hour. Fry in deep, hot fat until golden. Makes 20–24 balls.

*Matzah-Cheese Kugel

5 eggs	*sour cream or yogurt topping,*
1 cup milk	* if desired*
1/4 cup sugar	*1 tsp. cinnamon*
6 matzahs, broken into small	*3 T. butter, melted*
* pieces*	*salt, to taste*
1 lb. (1/2 K.) cottage cheese	

Beat eggs with milk. Combine with cottage cheese, salt, sugar, cinnamon and butter. In a greased 1 1/2 quart baking dish, arrange half the matzahs. Pour over matzahs half the cheese mixture, then remaining matzahs and cheese. Bake in 350° F (175° C) oven for 35 to 40 minutes or until mixture is set. Serves 6.

*Pesach "Lasagne"

2 whole matzahs
1 1/2 cups soft white cheese
salt, pepper and onion, to taste
butter

1/4 lb. (100 g.) hard cheese,
  sliced
1 large can tomato purée

Run one matzah under water on both sides until soft and
pliable. (Be careful not to let it get too soft.) Place in a 9 x 9-
inch square pan which has been buttered. Place 3/4 cup of the
soft white cheese on top, spreading evenly. Mix tomato sauce
and spices well. Spread half of this over cheese. Put half of hard
cheese over this. Repeat the process with the other half of the
ingredients. Bake in a medium oven for about 30 minutes. Slice
to serve.

*Matzahs and Cheese

1/2 lb. (250 g.) cottage cheese
1/2 tsp. salt
6 whole matzahs
dash of nutmeg

2 T. butter
5 eggs
1/2 tsp. cinnamon
1 tsp. sugar

Combine cheese, salt and 3 eggs, mixing well. Dip whole
matzahs in remaining 2 lightly beaten eggs. Place layer of
matzahs in a buttered dish. Cover with a layer of cheese and
sprinkle with mixture of cinnamon, nutmeg and sugar.
Alternate layers of matzahs and cheese until used up. Bake at
350°F (175°C) for 30 minutes.

Fried Eggs with Special Sauce

1 medium onion
1/4 red sweet pepper
8 eggs
1/2 cup tomato paste

salt and pepper, to taste
2 medium tomatoes
1 clove garlic (optional)
1 tsp. potato starch

Heat skillet with 1 T. oil. Brown onion. Drain oil and add
peeled, cubed tomatoes, chopped pepper, mashed garlic, salt,
pepper, tomato paste, potato starch and 3/4 cup water. Bring to
a boil and cook 5–7 minutes. Remove from heat. Fry eggs,
sunny-side up, in another pan. Pour sauce around eggs and
serve.

Egyptian Omelette

2 small eggplants, cubed
1 oz. (30 g.) butter or oil
1 medium onion, diced
8 eggs, beaten lightly

fresh black pepper, grated
1 clove garlic, crushed
salt, to taste

Place cubed eggplant in a strainer. Sprinkle with salt and leave for an hour. Rinse and dry with paper towels. Melt butter in large frying pan. Add onion and garlic and fry until onion is tender. Add cubed eggplant and fry until tender. Add eggs, salt and pepper to taste and stir. Lower the heat and cook for 20–25 minutes or until omelette is firm. Turn omelette over on a plate, slip back into pan to brown other side or place pan under grill until top is browned.

Spanish Omelette

3 T. olive oil
3 large potatoes, diced
6 eggs

salt, to taste
2 large onions, diced

Heat olive oil slowly in a medium-sized frying pan. Add potatoes and onions and season with salt. Cover the pan and cook vegetables on a low flame for 15–20 minutes, stirring frequently to prevent burning and adding oil if necessary. Beat eggs lightly. Add the soft, cooked vegetables, mixing quickly. Pour most of the oil out of the frying pan, leaving a thin layer only. Reheat the oil and pour in egg-vegetables mixture. Cook for 5 minutes, tilting pan occasionally to either side to prevent sticking. Place an oven-proof plate over the frying pan. Turn the omelette over onto the plate and slip back into pan to brown the second side. An alternative method is to place the pan under a grill until the omelette is firm and browned.
Variations: Add chopped spinach, mushrooms or parsley.

*Cheese-Stuffed Tomatoes

4 large tomatoes	*3 T. scallions, chopped*
1 1/4 cups yellow cheese,	*1/4 cup matzah meal*
grated	*4 T. butter, melted*

Wash tomatoes and cut in half crosswise. Hollow centers slightly. Mix together matzah meal, cheese and grated onions. Stuff tomatoes. Arrange in buttered dish and put a dab of butter on top of each. Bake in medium oven until tender.

Potato-Cheese Dish

2 lb. (1 K.) potatoes	*1/4 cup yellow cheese, grated*
1 cup cottage cheese	*2 tsp. salt*
2 T. parsley, chopped	*1/8 tsp. pepper*
1/4 cup onion, finely minced	*3/4 cup milk*

Dice potatoes and cook until tender. Drain and turn into a buttered baking dish. Combine cheese, onion, salt, pepper, milk and parsley. Pour over potatoes. Sprinkle with grated cheese. Bake at 400° F (200° C) for 15 minutes.

Spicy Eggplant Special

4 small eggplants	*8 oz. (200 g.) tomato paste*
2 tomatoes, diced	*2 cloves garlic*
2 onions, diced	*1 tsp. salt*
1 green pepper, chopped or	*1 tsp. pepper*
1 medium zucchini squash,	*1 1/2 tsp. sugar*
grated	

Cut ends off eggplants. Cook unpeeled in water. Sauté green pepper or squash, tomatoes and onions for 5–10 minutes. Add salt, pepper and tomato paste. Cook until soft. Scoop out inside of eggplants 2/3 of the way down. Dice and add to vegetables. Stuff eggplants, place in baking pan and pour the rest of the tomato paste over them. Bake for 1/3 hour or fry on a low fire. *Variation:* Place slices of cheese on top of eggplants, then pour tomato paste over them. Grate more cheese on top for decoration.

*Pesach Spinach Square

1 lb. (1/2 K.) spinach	*5 square matzahs*
1 1b. (1/2 K.) cottage cheese	*1 T. sour cream*
1/2 lb. (1/4 K.) yellow cheese, sliced	*5 eggs, separated*
	salt and pepper, to taste

Preheat oven to 350° F (175° C). Steam spinach 10 minutes. In a bowl, break up matzahs. Put spinach leaves in colander over matzah and let juice moisten pieces. Mix in spinach. In a separate bowl, beat egg yolks with cottage cheese, sour cream and salt. Fold whipped egg whites into yolks. Heat a 9-inch square glass dish 5 minutes in oven. Spread 1/2 of egg mixture in dish, top with sliced cheese and a layer of spinach mixture. Repeat until all is used up. Bake 45 minutes.

Farmer's Chop Suey

1/2 lb. (1/4 K.) soft cheese	*1–2 cups yogurt*
2 cups mixed fresh vegetables, diced	*salt and pepper, to taste*

Mix together all ingredients and serve. Instead of cheese and yogurt, 1 1/2 cups of sour cream may be substituted.

*Passover Pizza

2 eggs	*4–5 matzahs*
salt and pepper, to taste	*1/2 cup milk*
tomato sauce	*2 T. margarine or oil*
6 slices yellow cheese	*oregano*
1/4 cup yellow cheese, grated	

Beat eggs and milk with salt. Dip matzahs into mixture and let soak 5 minutes. Place on a greased cooked sheet with 1-inch sides. Cover with cheese, pour sauce over and add any herbs desired. Sprinkle with grated cheese. Bake in a preheated 375° F oven for 15–20 minutes. Allow to set for 2 minutes before cutting into squares, then serve while hot.

*Eggplant Casserole

1 medium eggplant	1 cup celery, diced
1/2 cup onion, chopped	1 T. butter
2 eggs	1 tsp. salt
1/4 tsp. pepper	1/4 cup matzah meal
1/4 cup yellow cheese, grated	

Boil eggplant in salt water 15–20 minutes. Drain and peel. Chop into small pieces. Sauté onion and celery in butter. Combine with eggplant. Add eggs, salt and pepper with 1/4 cup matzah meal. Place in well-buttered dish and spread cheese on top. Bake 35–40 minutes at 350° F (175° C).

*Creamy Potatoes

3 lb. (1 1/2 K.) potatoes	3 eggs
3/4 cup onions, chopped	1 1/2 tsp. salt
1 1/2 cups yellow cheese, grated	dash of pepper
1/2 cup matzah meal	1 1/2 cups sour cream

Sauté the onion. Cook potatoes until tender. Drain, peel and slice thin, arranging slices in buttered casserole dish. Combine cheese, matzah meal and onion. Spread over potatoes. Beat eggs, salt and pepper. Add sour cream. Pour over for topping. Bake 20 minutes at 350° F (175° C).

Pepper Potatoes

4 T. oil	salt, to taste
4 small onions, diced	1 cup sour cream
8 large potatoes, cooked	2 tsp. paprika
3 green or red sweet peppers, sliced	

Fry onions lightly in oil for a few minutes. Add peppers. Cube potatoes and season with paprika and salt. Fry lightly with onions and peppers. Pour on sour cream. Heat without boiling. Serve.

Delicious Potato-Egg Casserole

6 potatoes, sliced
6 hard-boiled eggs, sliced
3 cups sour cream
6 T. oil or butter
salt and pepper, to taste

Layer casserole with 1/3 of the potatoes, 2 eggs and 1 cup sour cream, sprinkling with salt and pepper and 2 T. oil. Repeat twice. Bake for 3 hours in a wonder pot or in a medium oven until potatoes are soft and casserole is done.

Vegetable-Cheese Spread

2 cups white cheese, 5% or 9%
1/4 cup sour cream
1/4 cup carrot, finely grated
1/4 cup radish, finely grated
1/4 cup green scallions
1/4 cup green or yellow pepper

Mix all ingredients. Coarsely blend vegetables in blender. Add to cheese cream.

Potato-Cheese Kugel

3 eggs
2 cups water
6 oz. potato pancake mix
1 lb. cottage cheese, 1/2% fat
3/4 cup yogurt, skim milk, or
  sour cream

Combine eggs, water and potato pancake mix as directed on package. Stir in cheese and yogurt. Pour into greased 8-inch square pan. Bake 1 hour at 350° F (175° C) or until the edges are browned. Serves 6.

Zucchini Casserole

2 medium zucchini, sliced
  diagonally
2 tomatoes, sliced
12 slices yellow cheese
1 large onion, thinly sliced
2 green peppers, sliced
salt and pepper, to taste
2 T. butter

Grease wonder pot and arrange half of the zucchini slices on the bottom. Add half of the onion, tomatoes and green pepper and 1/3 of the cheese slices. Sprinkle with salt and pepper, dot with half the butter. Repeat, using 1/3 more of the cheese. Bake 45–60 minutes or until vegetables are tender. Arrange the remaining 1/3 of the cheese slices on top and bake until cheese softens.

*Spinach-Cheese Kugel

2 packages frozen, chopped
    spinach
1 cup 1/2% white cheese, or
    yogurt
2 cups cottage cheese, lowfat

4 eggs or 6 whites, beaten
1 cup matzah meal
1 tsp. salt
1/2 tsp. nutmeg, optional

Defrost spinach. Add white cheese or yogurt and stir. Add the rest, reserving 1/2 cup matzah meal. Spread in greased 9 x 13-inch pan. Sprinkle with remaining matzah meal. Cover and bake 35 minutes at 375° F (175° C). Uncover and bake 10 minutes longer.

Spinach Souffle

2 packages chopped spinach,
    cooked
6 egg whites or 4 eggs

1 potato, cooked and grated
1 tsp. salt
2 cups cottage cheese, lowfat

Mix all ingredients. Put into greased baking dish. Bake at 350°F (175° C) for about 1 hour, or until firm.

*Leek, Potato & Matzah Gratin

1 red bell pepper, diced
1 cup hot water
6 oz. skim milk
2 large leeks, white part
    chopped
5 mushrooms, sliced

3 matzahs, broken
4 potatoes, baked, peeled and
    sliced
minced chives or green onions
salt, pepper and garlic, to taste

Preheat oven to 350° F (175° C). Add leeks to skillet and sauté in a little water, covering until softened. Add red pepper and sauté 5 minutes. Combine matzahs with water in bowl. Soak 3–5 minutes, until soft. Drain, squeeze out excess water. Combine leek mixture and matzahs with remaining ingredients, except chives. Stir until fully mixed. Pour into a lightly greased shallow 2-quart casserole. Sprinkle chives over top. Bake 35–40 minutes or until top is golden. Let stand 5–10 minutes and cut. Serves 4.

Complementary
Side Dishes

KUGELS AND LATKES

Yerushalmi Kugel
Grated Potato Kugel
*Matzah-Nut Kugel
*Mashed Potato Kugel
Potato and Meat Pudding
*Piquant Matzah Kugel
*Sweet Matzah Pudding
Vegetable Kugel
*Grated Carrot Pudding
*Carrot Kugel
*Rich Carrot Kugel
*Carrot-Nut Pudding
*Spinach Pie
Fruit and Nut Kugel
*Apple-Matzah Casserole
*Tomato-Onion Casserole

*Mediterranean Vegetable Casserole
*Zucchini Kugel
*Matzah Meal Pancakes
*Eggplant Latkes
Potato Latkes
Potato-Walnut Latkes
*Apple Pancakes
*Apple Latkes
*Cauliflower Latkes
*Zucchini Latkes
Yummy Potato Dough
  Knishes from Yerushalayim
*Potato Knishes
*Mock Potato Knishes
Super Duper Weinberg
  Potato Surprise Balls

VEGETABLES AND SALADS

Arabic Salad
Beet Preserves
Special Beets with Orange Juice
Beet Salad
Sweet-and-Sour Red Cabbage
Creamy Cabbage
Cole Slaw
Plum-Potato Tzimmes
Orange Juice Tzimmes
Special Tzimmes
Raw Carrot Salad
Carrot-Scallion Salad
Eggplant Salad
Scalloped Eggplant
*Eggplant Baked in Cheese Sauce
Green Salad with Lime Dressing
Romaine Lettuce Salad

*Stuffed Peppers (Pareve)
Green Pepper or Gamba Salad
Zucchini or Kohlrabi Salad
Zucchini Goulash
Sweet Potato Purée
Lebanese Potato Salad
Potato Salad
Pumpkin Pie
Pumpkin with Extra Ta'am
Tomato Salad
Stuffed Tomatoes
Waldorf Salad
Israeli Waldorf Salad
Vegetables with Sauce
Confetti Vegetables
Stir-Fried Vegetables
*Deep-Fried Vegetables

PICKLES

Dill Pickles
Pickled Cabbage — Sauerkraut

Marinated Peppers
Pickled Tomatoes

DRESSINGS

Chrein
Tomato Horseradish
Avocado Mayonnaise
One-Egg Mayonnaise
Rich Mayonnaise

Easy Mayonnaise
French Dressing
Tomato Sauce
Salad Dressing
Celery-Cheese Dressing

Kugels and Latkes

Yerushalmi Kugel

4 1/2 lb. (2 K.) potatoes

4 eggs

1 tsp. oil

salt, to taste

2 T. oil

Cook the peeled potatoes until tender but not soft. Drain and mash. Add eggs, oil and salt. Prepare a pot by spreading oil on sides and bottom. Heat. When oil is hot, pour in the potato mixture. Cook for at least 30 minutes on a small flame until sides are browned and kugel has risen in bulk. Cool until completely cold. Turn over. Cook on other side in same pot 15–30 minutes.

Grated Potato Kugel

3 cups potatoes, grated

3 T. onion, grated

4 T. oil

3 eggs

1 1/2 tsp. salt

1/8 tsp. pepper

1/3 cup potato starch

Beat eggs until thick. Stir in potatoes and rest of ingredients. Grease dish. Bake at 350°F (175° C) for 1 hour or until browned.

Variation: For Cheese Potato Kugel, add 1/2 lb. (250 g.) soft cheese.

*Matzah-Nut Kugel

3 matzahs

2 T. chicken fat

1 cup matzah meal

5 eggs, separated

1/2 cup almonds, chopped

rind of 1/2 lemon, grated

1/2 tsp. salt

1 large apple, grated

Soak matzahs in water and press out moisture. Melt 2 T. chicken fat in frying pan. Add matzahs and fry until somewhat dry. Remove to bowl and stir in matzah meal. Beat egg yolks and mix in almonds, lemon rind, salt and apple. Whip up whites and fold in. Bake in well-greased baking dish at 350° F (175° C) for 45 minutes. Pour hot chicken fat on top before baking.

*Mashed Potato Kugel

4 1/2 lb. (2 K.) potatoes, cooked and mashed	a little salt, to taste
2 T. matzah meal	6 eggs
	oil

Mix all ingredients well. Grease sides and bottom of pot with olive oil. Pour in potato mixture. Cook 30 minutes on a small flame. Cool. Turn over and cook 30 minutes on other side.

Potato and Meat Pudding

3 large cooked potatoes	salt and pepper, to taste
2 cups cooked chopped meat	6 eggs

Mash potatoes and add eggs one at a time. Beat well. Season with salt and pepper. Grease baking dish. Put in alternate layers of mashed potatoes and meat with mashed potatoes on top. Bake until brown.

*Piquant Matzah Kugel

1 cup minced onion	1 tsp. salt
1 cup finely diced celery	1/4 tsp. black pepper
6 T. chicken fat	2 tsp. paprika
6 matzahs, broken into small pieces	2 eggs, slightly beaten
	2 1/4 cups chicken soup

Sauté onions and celery in fat until onion is tender. Add broken matzahs. Combine remaining ingredients and add to matzah mixture. Pour into a well-greased 1/2-quart baking dish. Place in moderate oven, 375° F (190° C), and bake for 30 minutes or until firm. Serves 6–8.

*Sweet Matzah Pudding

6–8 matzahs	3/4 cup sugar
3 eggs	cinnamon
2 apples, grated	fruit juice

Soak matzahs in water until soft. Drain. Add eggs and fruit juice. Add sugar and cinnamon and grated apples. Bake in a 9 x 12-inch pan for 30–45 minutes at 350° F (175° C).

Vegetable Kugel

1 or 2 carrots, grated	salt, to taste
1 beet, grated	1 egg
1 potato, grated	potato starch (to bind)

Mix all ingredients together. Grease pan generously and bake for 30 minutes in hot oven.

★ Grated Carrot Pudding

1 lb. (1/2 K.) raw carrots, grated	1 tsp. salt
	1 tsp. oil
1 matzah, in crumbs	1 cup chicken broth
4 eggs, slightly beaten	4 tsp. parsley, finely chopped
1 tsp. onion, grated	

Preheat oven to 325° F (165° C). Combine all ingredients except 2 tsp. parsley and mix well. Pour into a well-greased 1 1/2-quart baking dish. Bake for 50 minutes or until firm. Garnish with rest of parsley.

★ Carrot Kugel

4 1/2 lb. (2 K.) carrots	6 eggs
2 T. matzah meal	1 tsp. sugar
1 tsp. salt	

Cook carrots, mash and drain well. Add in other ingredients and mix. Bake at 350° F (175° C) for 30 minutes or, cook 30 minutes on a small flame. Cool. Turn over and cook 30 minutes on other side. This kugel can be made without matzah meal, but must be cooled entirely before turning over.

★ Rich Carrot Kugel

8 medium carrots, scraped and grated	6 eggs, well beaten
	2 T. matzah meal
2 large apples, peeled and grated	1/2 cup potato starch
	1 cup sugar
peel of 1 lemon, grated	1/2 cup sweet red wine

Combine, place in well-greased 2-quart (2-liter) baking dish and bake in 375° F (190° C) oven u   l-browned, about 50–60 minutes. Makes 8 servings.

*Carrot-Nut Pudding

8 eggs, separated
1 1/2 cups confectioner's sugar
1/2 cup matzah meal
2 cups raw carrots, grated
1/2 cup almonds, ground
1/2 lemon rind, grated
1 T. wine
1/4 tsp. salt

Beat yolks until light. Stir in sugar and continue beating. Add matzah meal, carrots, almonds, lemon rind and wine. Mix thoroughly. Beat egg whites with salt until stiff and fold lightly into batter. Bake in a well-greased and slightly-floured baking pan at 300°F (150° C) for 1 hour.

*Spinach Pie

1 large onion, chopped
3 medium carrots, peeled and
  grated
1 package chopped spinach
2 eggs, well beaten
1/2 cup matzah meal
1 1/2 tsp. salt
1/8 tsp. pepper

Heat oven to 375° F (190° C). Cook the vegetables together in 1/2 cup water until spinach is defrosted. Drain, let cool 3 minutes. Stir in remaining items. Pour into a greased pie pan or 8 x 11-inch baking dish and bake 45 minutes. Makes 6 servings.

Fruit and Nut Kugel

2 large apples
1/2 cup walnuts (or other nuts)
1/4 cup honey
1/2 tsp. salt
2 T. sugar
1 T. lemon juice
1 T. lemon rind, grated
5 eggs
2–3 T. potato starch

Pare, core and slice apples. Line bottom of greased pan with apples. Beat yolks until light and frothy. Add honey, nuts, salt and sugar. Add lemon juice and rind. Fold in egg whites and potato starch. Pour over apples. Bake for 30 minutes in hot oven. (Can also be made without separating eggs.)

*Apple-Matzah Casserole

4 matzahs	1 cup chopped walnuts
3 eggs, beaten	3 apples, pared and sliced very
1/2 tsp. salt	thin
4 T. sugar	1/2 tsp. cinnamon
5 T. melted butter or oil	

Break matzahs into thin strips. Pour boiling water over them.
Drain and let cool. Stir in eggs, salt, sugar and butter or oil.
Pour 1/2 of mixture into well-greased casserole dish. Cover with
walnuts and apples. Sprinkle with cinnamon and sugar. Cover
with remaining matzah mixture. Dot with butter. Bake at
350°F (175° C) for 30 minutes.

*Tomato-Onion Casserole

4 onions, sliced	2 T. sugar or honey
4 cups canned stewed tomatoes	3 matzahs
1 tsp. salt (optional)	3 T. margarine or oil
1/4 tsp. pepper	

Line a 9 x 9-inch baking pan with slices of onion. In a bowl,
season tomatoes with salt, pepper and sugar or honey. Place a
few tomatoes on top of the onions, then a matzah. Repeat
twice, ending with the matzah. Dot with margarine or oil. Bake
at 375°F (190° C) for 30 minutes. Serves 8.

*Mediterranean Vegetable Casserole

4 matzahs	3 small ripe tomatoes, chopped
1-10 oz. box frozen spinach,	1 onion, finely chopped
cooked	12 oz. tomato sauce
2 cups cooked potatoes, cubed	1/2 cup chopped olives (op-
1 zucchini, grated	tional)

Lay 2 matzahs across the bottom of a long casserole dish. Then
add the following in layers: tomatoes, onions, zucchini,
potatoes, spinach and sauce. Repeat layers again, starting with
matzah. Bake 25 minutes at 375°F (190° C). Serves 8.

*Zucchini Kugel

3 or 4 zucchini, grated
1 very large onion, grated
1 egg

matzah meal
salt and pepper, to taste

After grating zucchini and onion, add salt, pepper, egg and matzah meal to mixture. Put into loaf pan and bake at 350° F (175° C) until firm and top is browned.

*Matzah Meal Pancakes

1/2 cup matzah meal
1/2 tsp. salt
1 tsp. sugar

3 eggs, separated
3/4 cup water or milk

Beat egg whites. Mix dry ingredients. Beat yolks and water. Combine dry ingredients and yolks. Let stand 15 minutes and fold in beaten whites. Drop by spoonfuls in hot, greased frying pan and serve after done with.sugar.

*Eggplant Latkes

1 large eggplant, peeled and
  cubed
1/2 cup matzah meal
1 onion, finely chopped

salt, pepper, parsley and garlic
  powder, to taste
tomato sauce
oil

Boil eggplant until very soft. Drain and mash. Add matzah meal, onions and spices. Mix well. Form into patties and fry on both sides until light brown. Serve covered with tomato sauce. Makes 12.

Potato Latkes

6 medium potatoes, peeled
1 small onion
2–3 eggs

3 T. potato starch
salt and pepper, to taste

Grate raw, peeled potatoes and onion. Drain in colander or strainer to remove liquid. Mix in eggs and other ingredients. Fry in hot oil, dropping by tablespoonfuls and flattening into pancakes. Brown on both sides. Place on paper towels to absorb excess oil. Serve hot. Delicious with applesauce or sour cream or sprinkled with sugar.

Potato-Walnut Latkes

2 oz. (50 g.) chicken fat
2 oz. (50 g.) oil
2 lb. (1 K.) cooked potatoes
4 eggs

1/2 cup chopped walnuts
2 tsp. salt
1/4 tsp. pepper

Melt fat in pan. Add oil and heat. Mash potatoes. Add eggs, walnuts, salt and pepper. Fry. Garnish with walnuts.

*Apple Pancakes

1 cup matzah meal
3 eggs, beaten
2 T. oil

3 tart apples, sliced
1/2 tsp. salt
1/2 cup water

Mix ingredients in order given. Drop by spoonfuls into deep, hot fat 375°F (190° C) and fry until golden brown, or fry as pancakes. Drain on paper toweling and sprinkle with cinnamon and sugar.

*Apple Latkes

4 apples, grated
6 T. matzah meal

1/2 tsp. cinnamon
oil

Mix apples, matzah meal and cinnamon together in a bowl. Spoon mixture into oiled frying pan and fry over medium heat for a few minutes. Flip over and cook a few more minutes on the other side.

*Cauliflower Latkes

2 cups cauliflower, cooked
2 T. matzah meal

2 eggs
salt and pepper, to taste

Chop cauliflower. Combine with rest. Form into patties and fry.

*Zucchini Latkes

2 medium zucchini
2 eggs

4 T. matzah meal
1 small onion

Grate squash and onion. Squeeze out excess liquid and add eggs and matzah meal. Fry in deep oil. Drain on paper towels.

Yummy Potato Dough
Knishes from Yerushalayim

3/4 cup fried onions
6 T. oil
4 cups mashed potatoes
1/2 cup potato starch

3 eggs
1 tsp. salt
1/4 tsp. pepper

Brown onions in 4 T. oil. Knead potatoes, remainder of oil, potato starch, eggs, salt and pepper. Break off into pieces and flatten slightly so they are approximately 4-inches square. Place 1 tsp. of browned onions on each and cover by pinching together. Place on greased baking sheet and bake at 375° F (190° C) for approximately 30 minutes.

⋆Potato Knishes

Dough:

1 1/2 cups matzah meal
4 T. potato starch

1 1/3 cups water

Mix ingredients together well and refrigerate for 15 minutes. Form into 2 balls. Roll out each ball to 1/4-inch thickness and cut into 3 x 5-inch squares.

Filling:

3 cups potatoes, cooked and
  mashed
1 large onion, chopped

1/4 tsp. each, paprika and pep-
  per
salt, to taste

Sauté onion in a little oil. Mix all ingredients together. Place about 1 1/2 T. filling in each square of dough. Fold in half and pinch closed. Place on greased baking pan and bake at 400° F (200° C) until light brown. Makes 8.

★Mock Potato Knishes

4 1/2 cups mashed potatoes	*3 tsp. salt*
3 eggs	*1 large onion*
1/2 cup matzah meal	*4 T. oil*
1/4 tsp. pepper	

Brown onion in fat and mix all ingredients except matzah meal. Shape into strips and roll in matzah meal. Bake at 400° F (200° C) oven for approximately 20 minutes. Serve as appetizer or side dish. For variety, use meat or liver in place of onions. Slice while hot.

Super Duper Weinberg Potato Surprise Balls

2 cups firmly-packed mashed potatoes	*salt and pepper, to taste*
1/2–3/4 cup potato starch	*meat or chicken pieces, cooked*

Mix together potatoes, potato starch, salt and pepper. Knead into a dough. Shape into balls. Place a piece of meat or chicken in the center of each. Deep fry.

Vegetables and Salads

Arabic Salad

2 lb. (1 K.) tomatoes
4 cloves garlic
1/2 hot pepper
1 green pepper

2 T. sugar
1/4 tsp. salt
1 T. oil

Grind together tomatoes, garlic, hot pepper and green pepper into a paste. Add sugar, salt and oil. Mix.

Beet Preserves

2 lb. (1 K.) beets, peeled
1 lb. (1/2 K.) sugar
3/4 cup water

juice of 1 lemon
2 oz. (50 g.) almonds, blanched
ginger

Boil sugar and water. Add beets and cook on medium heat for 1 hour. Add juice of lemon and cook for another hour. Allow the mixture to jell, then add nuts and ginger.

Special Beets with Orange Juice

3 beets, cooked
2 T. potato starch
2 T. honey (or sugar)
1 cup orange juice

2 tsp. lemon juice
peel of 1 orange, grated or
  2 T. orange jam

Mix potato starch, honey, orange juice and lemon juice together. Cook until thick and clear, stirring constantly. Mix in grated orange peel or orange jam. Slice beets thinly and mix them in. Serve hot or cold. Delicious!

Beet Salad

4 medium beets
juice of 1/2 lemon

salt, pepper and sugar, to taste

Use raw beets or cook beets for about 15 minutes until barely tender. Grate finely. Mix in lemon juice. Season with salt, pepper and sugar, if you like. Delicious plain. Serves 6.

Sweet-and-Sour Red Cabbage

3 T. butter
1/2 cup onion, chopped
8 cups red cabbage, shredded
1 apple, peeled and diced
1 cup water

3 T. apple vinegar
2 T. sugar
1 1/2 tsp. salt
1/4 tsp. pepper

Sauté onions in butter 5 minutes. Mix in the cabbage. Cover and cook 5 minutes. Add apple, water, vinegar, sugar, salt and pepper. Cover and cook again 30 minutes, stirring frequently.

Creamy Cabbage

2 T. butter
6 cups cabbage,
  finely shredded
1 cup water

1 cup sour cream
1 1/2 tsp. salt
1/2 tsp. pepper

Melt butter in a saucepan. Sauté the cabbage 5 minutes. Add the water, cover and cook 10 minutes on a low flame. Drain. Mix in the cream and spices. Cook 5 minutes longer.

Cole Slaw

6 cups cabbage,
  finely shredded
1 cup carrots, grated
1/2 cups green pepper,
  chopped

2/3 cups mayonnaise
2 T. sugar
1 1/2 tsp. salt
2 T. lemon juice

Toss well and chill before serving.

Plum-Potato Tzimmes

1/3 cup oil
1 cup onions, sliced
1 cup water
2 lb. (1 K.) potatoes, peeled
  and quartered

1 lb. (1/2 K.) prunes, rinsed
  and drained
1 tsp. salt
1/4 cup honey

Sauté onions until golden. Add potatoes, prunes, salt and water. Cover and simmer on small flame for 1 hour. Add honey. Stir and simmer for 1 hour longer. Stir occasionally. Serves 6.

Orange Juice Tzimmes

8 large carrots	4 T. oil
orange juice to cover	rind of 1 lemon, grated
4 T. honey or 1/3 cup sugar	dash of ginger
salt, to taste	

Slice carrots. Cover with orange juice. Boil 10 minutes. Add honey or sugar, salt and oil. Simmer gently for about an hour or until liquid is almost all absorbed and carrots are glazed. Sprinkle with lemon rind and ginger and simmer 5 minutes more.

Special Tzimmes

2 lb. (1 K.) carrots	2 T. oil
3 T. sugar	2 tsp. salt

Either grate or chop carrots into fine pieces. Combine all ingredients in saucepan. Simmer on small flame without water. When slightly brown, add a little water. Cook over low heat for about 2 hours.

Raw Carrot Salad

1 lb. (1/2 K.) carrots	1/3 cup oil
2 T. lemon juice	1/4 tsp. sugar
3 T. parsley	salt and pepper, to taste

Peel and grate carrots finely. Mix the oil and lemon juice together. Add the carrots and parsley. Season with salt and pepper. Add sugar if desired.

Carrot-Scallion Salad

2 lbs. (1 K.) carrots, grated	juice of 1 lemon
leaves of 1/2 lb. (1/4 K.) scallions, diced	a little salt
	1 tsp. olive oil

Mix together. Serve.

Eggplant Salad

1 eggplant	1 tsp. oil
1/4 lb. (100 g.) soft cheese	1 T. lemon juice
1 T. onion, chopped	salt, pepper and chopped
1/2 green pepper, chopped	garlic, to taste

Roast eggplant on fire. Peel. Mash. Add green pepper, cheese, garlic and onion to taste. Add oil and lemon juice. Season with salt and pepper.

Variation: Add hard-boiled eggs and mayonnaise instead of cheese.

Scalloped Eggplant

1 large eggplant	1 onion
1 green pepper	salt and pepper, to taste
1 lb. (1/2 K.) tomatoes	oil

Peel and cube eggplant. Sauté onions and green peppers. Add eggplant and tomatoes. Put in greased pan and bake or simmer on top of stove about 30 minutes until soft.

*Eggplant Baked in Cheese Sauce

2 lb. (1 K.) eggplant	1 cup milk
oil	1/2 cup cheese, grated
1 T. matzah meal	salt and pepper, to taste
1 egg	

Fry unpeeled, thick eggplant slices in very hot oil. Place slices in greased wonder pot and dust with matzah meal. Mix egg and milk, then add cheese, salt and pepper. Pour sauce over eggplant. Bake until soft and set in sauce.

Green Salad with Lime Dressing

1 lime	2 cups fresh spinach leaves, packed
1/2 cup mayonnaise	
1 T. honey	2 cups strawberries, halved
2 cups Boston lettuce, packed	1 cup oranges, sliced

Grate rind and squeeze juice from lime. Combine rind, lime juice, dressing and honey. Cover and chill. Toss remaining ingredients in a large bowl; drizzle with dressing mixture. Serves 4.

Romaine Lettuce Salad

2 romaine lettuce, cut into
small pieces
juice of 3 lemons

salt, to taste
leaves of 1 scallion, diced

Combine all ingredients and toss.

* Stuffed Peppers (Pareve)

4 large peppers
2 tsp. margarine or oil
3/4 cup matzah farfel or
2 pieces of matzah, crushed
1/2 cup raisins

1 stalk celery, chopped
1 carrot, grated
1 T. dry red wine or apple
juice

Sauté farfel, raisins, celery, carrots and wine or juice for 10–15 minutes. Remove tops and seeds of peppers and stuff peppers with the mixture. Bake in a baking dish at 350°F (175° C) for 30 minutes or until soft. Add water if necessary, to prevent drying out. Serves 4.

Green Pepper or Gamba Salad

4 ripe green or red sweet
peppers
salad dressing

fresh mint, chopped and/or
fresh dill, chopped

Cut peppers into thin strips or grind. Mix with salad dressing, mint and/or dill.

Zucchini or Kohlrabi Salad

2 zucchini squash or
2 kohlrabi

salad dressing
dill or onion, chopped

Grate squash or kohlrabi finely or coarsely. Mix with salad dressing. Add chopped dill or onion. Toss.

Zucchini Goulash

2 lb. (1 K.) zucchini squash
1 lb. (1/2 K.) tomatoes
1 lb. (1/2 K.) onions

salt and pepper, to taste
chopped garlic
o

Cook squash, tomatoes and onions in small amount of water until soft. Season with salt, pepper and chopped garlic.

Sweet Potato Purée

1 1/2 lb. (750 g.) potatoes   1 tsp. salt
2 lb. (1 K.) sweet potatoes   pepper, to taste
4 T. oil or butter

Preheat oven to 400°F (200° C). Bake the white potatoes for 1 hour and the sweet potatoes for 45 minutes. Scoop out the pulp with a spoon and mash. Reheat mashed potatoes in a saucepan and stir in oil or butter. Season with salt and pepper. Serves 4–6.

Lebanese Potato Salad

4 large potatoes   1/4 cup lemon juice
1/2 cup fresh parsley, chopped   1 tsp. salt
1/4 cup green onions, finely   2 garlic cloves, minced
  chopped   1 dash pepper
1/4 cup olive oil

Peel, boil and cube potatoes. Mix in parsley and onions. Combine oil and seasonings and toss with rest of ingredients.

Potato Salad

3–4 potatoes   mayonnaise
1 small onion, chopped

Boil and cube potatoes. Add mayonnaise and onion to potatoes. Season to taste.
Variation: Add 1 large carrot, grated, and/or 2 hard-boiled eggs.

Pumpkin Pie

3 eggs   1/2 tsp. ginger (optional)
1 1/2 cups pumpkin, cooked   1/2 tsp. nutmeg
1 cup sugar   1 tsp. vanilla
1/2 tsp. salt   1 1/2 cups orange juice
1 1/2 tsp. cinnamon

Beat eggs. Add all ingredients until well blended. Pour into greased dish. Bake at 450° F (225° C) for 10 minutes and then at 350°F (175° C) for 45 minutes longer or until set.

Pumpkin with Extra Ta'am

1 lb. (1/2 K.) pumpkin	*salt, to taste*
1 onion, diced	*2 T. oil*

Cut pumpkin into small squares. Cook with onion, salt, oil and a little water until all the water is absorbed. Cool. Serve with meat.

Tomato Salad

4 tomatoes	*1 green pepper*
1 small radish	*1 small onion*
1 carrot	*2 T. olive oil*
1 cucumber	*a little salt*

Cut vegetables into small pieces. Add oil and salt. Toss.

Stuffed Tomatoes

4 large tomatoes	*1/2 bunch scallions, finely*
1 cucumber, finely diced	*chopped*
1 cup olives, chopped	*salt and pepper, to taste*

Scoop out pulp of tomatoes. Mix remaining ingredients together and stuff tomatoes. Serve chilled. Serves 4.

Waldorf Salad

1 cup apples, diced	*1 T. lemon juice*
1 cup celery, diced	*mayonnaise, sour cream*
1/4 cup nuts, chopped	*or yogurt, to taste*

Core and dice apples. Sprinkle with lemon juice. Add celery and nuts. Stir in mayonnaise, sour cream or yogurt. Serve cold. *Variation:* Omit mayonnaise. Prepare 1 package gelatin and stir in remaining ingredients. Chill in individual serving dishes.

Israeli Waldorf Salad

1 grapefruit	*1/3 cup almonds, chopped*
2 oranges	*2 cups cabbage, sliced thin*
2 apples	*dash of salt*
1 1/2 cups celery, diced	*3/4 cup mayonnaise*

Remove membranes from citrus fruit sections. Dice apples, chop celery and nuts and grate cabbage. Mix fruits and vegetables together. Add salt and mayonnaise and toss.

Vegetables with Sauce

2 cups vegetables   2–3 eggs
1 cup sour cream   3 T. potato starch

Cook a combination of vegetables. Make sauce by mixing eggs
with sour cream and adding potato starch. Pour over vegetables.
Steam or bake for 10 minutes. Serves 4.

Confetti Vegetables

2 1/2 T. butter   1 1/2 cups carrots, shredded
1 1/2 tsp. sugar   1 1/2 cups parsnips or turnips,
1 tsp. salt   shredded
2 1/4 cups zucchini, shredded

Cook zucchini, carrots and parsnips in large pot with 1/4–1/2
cup boiling water, adding butter, sugar and salt. Cover. Cook
about 5 minutes until vegetables are tender-crisp, stirring
occasionally.

Stir-Fried Vegetables

In large, oiled frying pan stir-fry chopped vegetables, including
carrots, celery, cauliflower, broccoli, tomatoes, onions, etc. until
soft. Season. Serves 4.
Serving suggestion: Pour over mashed potatoes.

*Deep-Fried Vegetables

1/2 cup water   2–3 medium zucchini,
2 T. potato starch   chopped, or
3/4 cup matzah meal   1 lb. mushrooms, sliced, or
salt and pepper, to taste   4 tomatoes, sliced

Mix together water and potato starch. Dip vegetables in
mixture, then in matzah meal. Deep fry in oil until tender.
Serve with tomato sauce. Serves 4–6.

Pickles

Dill Pickles

25 small cucumbers
3 stalks fresh dill
3 cloves fresh garlic
3 chili peppers (optional)

9 T. coarse salt
9 cups water
3 T. vinegar (optional)

Add cucumbers and pack into jars. Top each jar with garlic, dill and chili pepper. Mix water, salt and vinegar. Bring to boil. Cool slightly and pour over cucumbers. Be sure to cover. Add more water and salt, if necessary. Ready in a few days.

Pickled Cabbage — Sauerkraut

5 lb. (2 1/2 K.) cabbage
coarse salt

water

Finely shred cabbage. Pack into jars with a sprinkling of salt as you layer the cabbage. Pack in as tightly as possible. Add boiling water to cover. Close jars. Each day add salt and water as water diminishes. Ready in a few days.

Marinated Peppers

16 green and red sweet
  peppers
salt and pepper, to taste

4 T. oil
1 cup wine vinegar
garlic and sugar, to taste

Roast peppers over fire and broil until just charred. Turn over and char on other side. Rinse in cold water and remove skins. Put in bowl seeds, stem and all. Sprinkle with salt and pepper. Mix vinegar, garlic, sugar and oil. Pour over peppers. Ready in a few hours.

Pickled Tomatoes

20 green firm tomatoes,
*   medium sized*
1/2 cup salt
6 cups water
2/3 cup wine vinegar

4 cloves garlic
10 clove pieces
3 T. sugar
fresh dill

Wash tomatoes. Pack into jars. Bring other ingredients to a boil. Cool. Pour over tomatoes, making sure to cover them with the solution. Put dill on top. Close tight. Keep tomatoes covered with brine at all times, adding water, if necessary. If scum appears, skim. Will be ready in about a week.

Dressings

Chrein

1/2 cup fresh horseradish,
   grated
1/2 cup citrus vinegar
1 tsp. salt

2 cups beets, boiled
2 T. sugar
pinch of pepper

Blend all ingredients in blender. Refrigerate.

Tomato Horseradish

4 large, raw tomatoes
4-inch horseradish root
1 tsp. sugar

1/2 tsp. salt
2 T. lemon juice

Mash tomatoes fine and grate horseradish or put through blender. Add salt, sugar and lemon juice and mix well. Refrigerate. A bit sharp, but delicious.

Avocado Mayonnaise

2 large, very ripe avocados
2 T. mayonnaise
2 T. sour cream or yogurt
3 T. lemon juice
1 tsp. salt

3 T. oil
a dash of pepper
1/2 tsp. sugar
1 clove garlic, crushed

Peel avocados and take out pits. Cut into quarters. Blend with all other ingredients in a blender until a smooth mixture is formed — about 30 seconds. This can be done by hand by mashing the avocados with a fork. Add all other ingredients gradually. Season according to taste. Pour into a serving dish, cover well and chill.

One-Egg Mayonnaise

1 egg
1–1 1/2 cups olive oil

juice of 1/2 lemon
a little salt

Beat egg very well, adding olive oil one drop at a time until thick. Add lemon juice and salt. This should make about half a medium jar of mayonnaise.

Rich Mayonnaise

1 raw egg yolk
yolk of 1 boiled egg
1/2–1 cup oil
1 cup boiling water

1 T. potato starch
1/2 cup lemon juice
salt, pepper and sugar, to taste

Add cooked egg yolk to raw one. Mix well. Mix water with potato starch for 1 minute. Add everything together, mixing constantly, in blender.

Easy Mayonnaise

1 egg yolk
2 tsp. boiling water

1/2 cup oil

Beat together egg yolk with boiling water. Slowly and gradually, beat in 1/2 cup oil.

To stretch mayonnaise: Boil 2 cups water taken from vegetables or vegetable soup with 1 T. potato starch for 2–3 minutes. Cool. Blend into mayonnaise.

French Dressing

8 tomatoes
1 1/2 tsp. salt
1/3 cup honey
1 tsp. paprika

1/2 cup lemon juice
3 T. vinegar
2 T. onion, grated

Combine all the above ingredients, and then add 3/4 cup oil and 2 fresh cloves garlic, minced.

Tomato Sauce

4 1/2 lb. (2 K.) tomatoes
2 whole cloves garlic

1 tsp. salt
2 T. sugar

Grind tomatoes. Bring to a boil with whole garlic cloves, then simmer on a small flame for 30 minutes. Mix occasionally to avoid sticking. This should become a thick mixture. Remove garlic cloves and pour into a jar. Add 1 tsp. of oil and cover. This keeps in refrigerator at least a week and can be used as a sandwich spread or instead of commercial tomato purée in most recipes.

Salad Dressing

2 cups olive oil   1/2 tsp. salt
1 cup vinegar   pepper, to taste
1 large onion, minced   2 tsp. sugar

Combine all ingredients and shake well. Can keep refrigerated indefinitely.

Celery-Cheese Dressing

4 stalks celery, chopped   salt and pepper, to taste
1–2 small onions, chopped   1 tsp. lemon juice
butter   1 tsp. parsley, chopped
1 1/2 cups soft cheese   (optional)

Fry celery and onions in oil until almost soft. Remove from heat. Add cheese and other ingredients while warm.
Serving suggestion: Pour over baked potato halves.

Cakes & Cookies

───────────────── CAKES ─────────────────

*Matzah Meal Chocolate Cake
Pesach Chocolate Cake
Mocha Chocolate Cake
*Honey Cake
*Matzah Meal Banana Cake
Pesach Banana Cake
*Wine Cake I
Wine Cake II
Cooked Carrot Cake
Carrot Cake like Bubby Makes
*Apple Cake
*Special Passover Cake
Nut Cake
Super Duper Delicious Walnut Cake
Almond Nut Cake with
  Lemon Filling
*Orange-Nut Cake

*Orange Cake
*Torte
*Chocolate-Nut Torte
*Matzah Meal Sponge Cake
*Spicy Sponge Cake
Pesach Sponge Cake
*Cheese or Apple Cake
Chiffon Cake
*Jelly Roll
*Prune Upside-Down Cake
Brownie Cake
Chocolate Pie
Shavuos Cheese Cake on Pesach
*Pesach Lemon Pie
*Cream Puffs with Pesach
  Lemon Pie Filling
*Apple Pie

───────────────── COOKIES ─────────────────

*Chocolate Chip Cookies
*Almond Cookies
*Chameleon Cookies
*Coconut Macaroons
Coconut Cookies
Almond Macaroons
*Raisin and Nut Cookies
Meringues
Chocolate Nut Meringues
Fruit-Filled Meringue Cups
*Fruit-Filled Chremsels
*Chremsels

Pesach Brownies
*Easy Brownies
*Chocolate Bars
*Thumbprint Cookies
*Mocha Nut Bars
Pesach Muffins
*Potato Cupcakes
*Jelly Squares
*Easy Passover Bagels
*Chocolate Matzah Bars
*Mandelbroit

Cakes

*Matzah Meal Chocolate Cake

7 eggs, separated	1 cup sugar
4 T. cocoa	3/4 cup matzah meal
2 T. cold water	1/2 tsp. salt
1 orange (juice and rind)	1/2 cup nuts, chopped

Beat egg whites until stiff. Beat yolks, adding other ingredients. Fold in whites. Bake 45 minutes at 325°F (165° C) in ungreased rectangular pan. Let cool in oven.

Pesach Chocolate Cake

9 eggs, separated	1 cup sugar
8 oz. (200 g.) nuts, ground	1 tsp. vanilla or rum
8 oz. (200 g.) bittersweet chocolate	(or 1 T. red wine)

Beat whites until stiff. Beat yolks and sugar 10 minutes. Add cooled, melted chocolate and nuts. Fold all ingredients together. Bake at 350°F (175° C) for 40 minutes.

Mocha Chocolate Cake

8 eggs	1 cup sugar
3/4 cup potato starch	1 cup cocoa
1/4 cup strong coffee	1/4 tsp. salt

Separate whites and yolks. Beat whites stiff and add 1/2 cup sugar. Sift potato starch and cocoa three times. Beat yolks well. Add 1/2 cup sugar, coffee and salt. While stirring, add potato starch and cocoa. Fold in whites. Bake in a greased tube pan for 1 hour at 325°F (165° C). Invert pan on the neck of a bottle until cool.

*Honey Cake

3 eggs, separated	3/4 cup honey
1/2 cup potato starch	1/2 cup cake meal
1/2 tsp. ginger	1/4 tsp. salt
1/2 cup sugar	2/3 cup strong coffee
1/3 cup nuts, chopped	1/2 tsp. cinnamon

Beat egg whites stiff. Beat yolks, adding all other ingredients. Fold into whites. Turn out into a loaf pan and bake at 350°F (175° C) until a toothpick comes out clean or cake springs back to the touch.

*Matzah Meal Banana Cake

7 eggs, separated	1 cup sugar
1/4 tsp. salt	1 cup mashed bananas
3/4 cup matzah meal	1/4 cup potato starch
1/2–1 cup nuts, chopped	

Beat egg whites stiff. Beat yolks and sugar together, adding bananas, matzah meal, potato starch and salt. Fold in stiffly beaten whites last, along with nuts. Bake at 325° F (165° C) for 45 minutes in a lightly greased pan. Ice with the following frosting.

Frosting:

3 T. cold water	pinch of salt
1 egg white	7/8 cup sugar

Beat egg white until stiff. Heat remaining ingredients on low flame until sugar dissolves entirely. Slowly pour syrup into egg white while beating constantly. When slightly cool, frost cake.

Pesach Banana Cake

7 eggs, separated	1 cup sugar
1 cup mashed bananas	3/4 cup potato starch
1/4 tsp. salt	

Beat egg yolks. Add sugar and salt slowly, beating constantly until lemon colored. Add bananas and potato starch while beating. Fold in stiffly beaten egg whites. Bake in tube pan for 45 minutes at 350° F (175° C).

⋆ Wine Cake I

10 eggs, separated	2 cups sugar
1 cup matzah cake meal	1 cup nuts, chopped
1/2 cup wine	

Beat yolks until lemon colored. Add sugar and beat well. Add matzah cake meal together with nuts. Add wine and fold in stiffly beaten whites. Bake in ungreased tube pan 40–45 minutes at 325° F (165° C). Invert on neck of a bottle until cool.

Wine Cake II

7 eggs, separated	1 cup sugar
1/4 cup wine	1 cup chopped nuts
1/2 cup potato starch	

Beat whites stiff. Beat yolks well. Add all ingredients slowly to yolks while beating continuously. Gently fold in whites. Bake at 325° F (165° C) for 1 1/4 hours.

Cooked Carrot Cake

9 eggs	1 1/2 cups cooked carrots, mashed
1 T. orange juice	
2 1/2 cups ground almonds or 1/2 cup potato starch	1 3/4 cups sugar
	1 T. wine

Separate eggs. Beat yolks. Gradually add sugar to yolks. Beat until thick. Stir in carrots, orange juice, wine and almonds (or potato starch). Fold in stiffly beaten egg whites. Bake at 325° F (165° C) for 50 minutes.

Carrot Cake like Bubby Makes

1 large carrot	1 1/2 cups sugar
8 eggs, separated	2 cups nuts
juice of 1 lemon	

Peel and grate carrot. Add chopped nuts, lemon juice and sugar to beaten egg yolks. Add carrot. Beat whites stiffly. Fold into yolk batter. Bake in lightly greased pan for 30 minutes at 350° F (175° C).

*Apple Cake

Batter:
3 eggs
3/4 cup sugar
1/2 cup oil

3/4 cup matzah meal
1/2 cup potato starch

Filling:
3 green apples, finely sliced
1/2 tsp. cinnamon

1 tsp. sugar

Mix batter ingredients together and pour half into baking pan. Cover with apple mixture and then cover with remaining batter. Bake at 350° F (175° C) for 45 minutes, or until firm.

*Special Passover Cake

12 eggs, separated
1 1/2 cups sugar
1 1/2 cups matzah meal
1 cup oil
juice of 1 lemon, strained

1 1/2 cups nuts, ground
2–3 bananas, mashed
1 pkg. baking powder
1 pkg. vanilla sugar or
* 1 tsp. vanilla*

Preheat oven to 300° F (150° C). Beat yolks with 1/2 cup sugar until thick. Mix in oil, lemon juice, bananas, baking powder and vanilla. Blend in matzah meal and nuts. Beat whites until stiff, adding 1 cup sugar gradually. Fold first mixture very carefully into second. Line a large baking pan with aluminum foil. Grease lightly. Pour in mixture. Bake for 1 hour or until top browns.

Nut Cake

10 eggs, separated
3/4 lb. (300 g.) of nuts, finely
* ground*

1 tsp. vanilla
1 cup sugar

Beat yolks with sugar until light and creamy. Add nuts and vanilla. Fold in stiffly beaten egg whites. Turn out into a well-oiled tube pan and bake for 1 hour (or longer) at 350° F (175° C).

Super Duper Delicious Walnut Cake

10 egg whites   2 cups sugar
2 cups walnuts, crushed 2 tsp. rum (optional)
1/2 cup oil   5 T. cocoa

Beat egg whites until stiff. Gradually add sugar, then nuts, rum, oil and cocoa. Spread in two lined jelly roll pans. Bake at 320° F (160° C) for 1 hour (until crispy). Turn out on wax paper and cool. This cake is very thin but excellent.
Top with the following icing:

Icing:
10 yolks   2 cups sugar
2 tsp. vanilla

Beat yolks, sugar and vanilla. Cook in double boiler for 50 minutes. Spread half of slightly cooled icing on 1 layer of cake. Place other layer on top. Pour remaining icing over this. Refrigerate. Cut into strips.

Almond Nut Cake with Lemon Filling

8 eggs, separated   juice of 1 lemon
1/2 lb. (200 g.) almonds, finely   1 1/4 cups sugar
  ground

Beat egg yolks until thick. Add sugar. Fold in stiffly beaten whites, ground almonds and lemon juice. Bake in layer pans at 350° F (175° C) for 45 minutes.

Filling:
2 eggs   juice of 1 lemon
3/4 cup sugar   1 tsp. oil
1 T. potato starch   1 cup water

Mix sugar and potato starch together. Beat eggs well. Slowly add the sugar-potato starch mixture. Mix water, oil and lemon juice. Add to egg mixture. Cook in double boiler until thick, mixing constantly. Cool before spreading between layers. Sprinkle top with powdered sugar and chopped nuts or spread extra filling on top.

★ Orange-Nut Cake

8 eggs, separated
1 cup sugar
1 1/4 cup matzah cake meal
2/3 cup orange juice

1 tsp. orange rind, grated
1/2 tsp. cinnamon
1/4 tsp. salt
1/3 cup nuts, finely chopped

Beat yolks with 1/2 cup sugar and blend in orange juice and rind. Sift matzah cake meal, cinnamon and salt together. Stir in nuts. Mix into yolk mixture. Beat egg whites with remaining sugar until stiff. Carefully fold in beaten egg whites. Pour into ungreased 10-inch tube pan. Bake at 325° F (165° C) for 1 hour.

★ Orange Cake

3/4 cup cake meal
1 1/2 cups sugar
1 cup orange juice
pinch of salt

3/4 cup potato starch
6 egg yolks
1 cup egg whites

Sift cake meal and potato starch together three times. Add 1 cup sugar and sift again into a large bowl. Make a well in the center, drop in the egg yolks and mix. Add orange juice and grated rind and beat until smooth. Beat egg whites with salt until stiff. Add sugar to whites and continue to beat until smooth. Fold into batter and pour into ungreased tube pan or 2 layer pans. Bake 1 1/4 hours at 325° F (165° C).

★ Torte

6 eggs, separated
1/2 cup matzah meal
1/2 cup potato starch
1–3 T. oil

a little cinnamon
1 1/4 cups sugar
lemon rind

Beat egg whites stiff, adding sugar gradually. Mix all other ingredients with yolks. Fold in whites slowly. Bake in lightly greased wonder pot sprinkled with potato starch at 350° F (175° C). Check after 30 minutes with toothpick; it may take another 15–30 minutes to bake. Can be made using 1 cup matzah meal or 1 cup potato starch alone.

⋆ Chocolate-Nut Torte

4 oz. (120 g.) semi-sweet
  chocolate, grated
2 sweet apples, peeled and
  grated

6 eggs, separated
1 cup walnuts, chopped
1 1/2 cups sugar
1/2 cup matzah meal

Preheat oven to 350° F (175° C). Beat egg yolks with sugar until lemon colored and thick. Gently stir in walnuts, chocolate, apples and matzah meal. Beat egg whites until they form stiff peaks, but are not dry. Fold gently but thoroughly into egg yolk mixture. Pour into a 9-inch springform pan and bake for 45 minutes to 1 hour. Cool in pan before serving. Sprinkle with confectioner's sugar.

⋆ Matzah Meal Sponge Cake

8 eggs, separated
1/2 cup matzah cake meal
1/2 cup potato starch
1/2 tsp. almond extract

1 1/2 cups sugar
1 tsp. vanilla
1/4 tsp. salt

Beat yolks until light. Gradually add sugar, beating until fluffy. Mix and sift cake meal and potato starch. Fold into egg mixture, adding extracts. Beat whites with salt until stiff, but not dry. Fold lightly into batter. Bake in ungreased tube pan at 325° F (165° C) for 1 1/4 hours. Allow to cool in inverted pan.

⋆ Spicy Sponge Cake

8 eggs, separated
3/4 cup matzah meal
rind of 1 lemon, grated
1 cup almonds, chopped
1 tsp. allspice
1 1/2 cups confectioner's sugar

2 oz. (60 g.) chocolate, grated
2 tsp. cinnamon
juice of 1 orange
3 T. wine
1/2 tsp. salt

Sift matzah meal well. Beat yolks and confectioner's sugar until creamy. Add remaining ingredients, except whites and salt. Beat whites and salt stiff and fold into rest of batter. Turn into pan lined with wax paper and bake at 325° F (165° C) for 1 hour.

Pesach Sponge Cake

9 eggs, separated
juice of 1 lemon
3/4 cup sugar

1 scant cup potato starch,
*   sifted*

Beat egg yolks well. Add sugar slowly. Add lemon juice and beat thoroughly. Add potato starch and beat again. Fold in stiffly beaten egg whites and bake at 350° F (175° C) for 40–50 minutes.

*Cheese or Apple Cake

Dough:
1 1/2 cups matzah meal
1/2 cup oil or butter
1 egg
vanilla or lemon rind

1 cup potato starch
1/4 cup sugar
a little milk or fruit juice

Mix all ingredients to make a dough. Line wonder pot with 3/4 of dough. Fill with Cheese or Apple Filling, discussed below. Decorate with strips of remaining dough. Bake for 45 minutes to 1 hour on medium flame.

Cheese Filling:
1/2 lb. (250 g.) soft cheese
1–1 1/2 cups sugar, to taste
2 eggs

3–4 T. milk
vanilla

Mix together all the above for filling.

Apple Filling:
4–6 medium apples
1/2 cup sugar

1 tsp. cinnamon

Peel, core and dice apples thin. Mix in cinnamon and sugar.
Variation: Place all the dough in wonder pot and top with Cheese or Apple Filling.

Chiffon Cake

10 eggs, separated	*1 1/2 cups sugar*
1/4 cup oil	*1/4 cup orange juice*
juice of 1/2 lemon	*8 T. potato starch*

Beat egg whites until stiff. Add all ingredients to beaten yolks except potato starch, blending well. Slowly sprinkle potato starch 1 T. at a time over batter. Blend well. Fold in whites. Pour into lightly greased pan and bake at 350° F (175° C) for 45 minutes.

*Jelly Roll

6 eggs, separated	*1/4 tsp. salt*
3/4 cup sugar	*2 tsp. lemon juice*
1/2 cup matzah cake meal	*1/4 cup potato starch*
jelly	

Beat egg yolks. Add sugar and remaining ingredients, except for egg whites. Beat whites stiff and fold in. Bake at 375° F (190° C) for 12–15 minutes in shallow rectangular pan. Turn out on towel sprinkled with confectioner's sugar. When cool, spread jelly over cake and roll up.

*Prune Upside-Down Cake

1 lb. (1/2 K.) prunes, stewed	*6 egg yolks*
1 cup sugar	*1 T. lemon peel, grated*
1 T. lemon juice	*1/2 tsp. salt*
3/4 cup matzah cake meal	*6 egg whites*

Drain pitted prunes and reserve juice. Line bottom of tube pan with baking paper. Arrange prunes on paper. Combine yolks, sugar, lemon peel, juice and salt. Beat until thick. Gently fold in matzah cake meal. Beat whites until stiff and gently fold together. Spread batter over prunes. Bake at 350° F (175° C) about 40 minutes. Cool cake before removing from pan.

Brownie Cake

8 eggs
2 1/2 cups sugar
1 1/2 cups oil

1 cup cocoa
1 1/2 cups potato starch

Combine eggs, sugar and oil. Add cocoa and potato starch and mix well. Heat a greased wonder pot for 10 minutes. Pour batter into wonder pot and bake 1 1/4 hours. Do not turn over to cool.

Chocolate Pie

Crust:
A thin layer of spongecake.

Filling:
5 oz. bittersweet chocolate
3 T. water

4 eggs, separated
2 T. sugar

Melt chocolate and water in saucepan. Let cool and add yolks. Mix well. Beat whites, adding sugar. Fold egg whites into chocolate mixture. Pour over crust and refrigerate until set.

Frosting:
1 cup sugar
1/3 cup water

dash of salt
2 egg whites

Combine sugar, water and salt in pan and bring to a boil. Beat egg whites until stiff and slowly add sugar mixture to whites. Beat 7 minutes and spread on top.

Shavuos Cheese Cake on Pesach

3 lbs. (1 1/4 K.) soft cheese
1–1 1/2 cups heavy sour cream
1 3/4 cups sugar
3/4 tsp. salt

6 eggs
2 T. orange juice
3–3 1/2 T. potato starch

Mix sugar, potato starch, salt and orange juice. Gradually blend in cheese. Add eggs, one at a time. Blend 1/2 to 1 cup sour cream into batter. Bake in wonder pot for approximately 1 hour till set. Then add another 1/2 cup of sour cream on top and cook for another 5 minutes.

*Pesach Lemon Pie

Crust:

1 cup matzah meal   1/4 cup shortening
pinch of salt   pinch of cinnamon
1 tsp. sugar

Combine all ingredients. Line a medium pie plate with mixture.
Bake 10 minutes at 375° F (190° C).

Filling:

juice of 2 lemons   1 1/2 cups water
rind of 1 lemon, grated   3 eggs, separated
1 cup sugar   3 T. potato starch

Preheat oven to 325° F (165° C). Boil lemon juice, rind and 1/2
cup of sugar in 1 cup of water. Allow to cool, then stir in yolks.
Moisten potato starch with 1/2 cup water and blend in. Let
cook 10 minutes, until blended and creamy. Beat egg whites
with remaining 1/2 cup sugar. Quickly fold 1/2 of beaten whites
into the yolk mixture. Use remaining whites to top the pie, in
swirls or peaks. Bake immediately until slightly brown.

*Cream Puffs with Pesach Lemon Pie Filling

1/2 cup oil   1 tsp. salt
1 cup boiling water   4 eggs
1 cup matzah cake meal   chocolate syrup

Mix oil, water, matzah cake meal and salt well. Add eggs, one
at a time. Beat until smooth. Drop on a greased and floured
cookie sheet. Bake at 425° F (210° C) for 10 minutes and then
at 350° F (175° C) for an additional 20–25 minutes. When cool,
fill with Pesach Lemon Pie Filling (see recipe above) and cover
with chocolate syrup.

⋆ Apple Pie

Crust:

6 eggs

1 cup oil

2 tsp. potato starch

2 cups sugar

2 cups matzah meal

pinch of salt

Filling:

4 or more apples, sliced

3/4 cup sugar

2 tsp. cinnamon

juice of 1 lemon

Topping:

1/2 cup nuts

2 tsp. cinnamon

1/2 cup sugar

Peel and slice apples. Soak in sugar, cinnamon, lemon juice mixture. Mix ingredients for crust. Spread half in greased pan. Pour apples and juice over. Cover with remaining crust. Sprinkle on topping. Bake at 350° F (175° C) for 1–1 1/4 hours.

Cookies

*Chocolate Chip Cookies

1 cup matzah farfel (finely broken-up matzahs)
3/4 cup sweet chocolate pieces, chopped
1 cup matzah meal
1/2 cup walnuts, chopped
3/4 cup sugar
2 eggs
1/3 cup oil

Mix all ingredients, chill if time allows, and roll into 3/4-inch balls. Bake at 350°F (175° C) for 30 minutes.

*Almond Cookies

1/2 cup matzah cake meal
1/8 tsp. salt
1/2 cup sugar
1/4 cup potato starch
1/4 cup almonds, chopped
2 eggs, beaten

Sift potato starch, cake meal and salt together. Add remaining ingredients and mix well. Roll out on a floured board and cut into desired shapes. Bake on greased sheet at 400° F (200° C) 8–10 minutes.

*Chameleon Cookies

2 eggs
3/4 cup sugar
1/2 cup oil
juice of 1/2 orange
1 cup matzah cake meal
1 cup potato starch
1/2 tsp. salt

Mix all ingredients together and chill. Drop by the teaspoonful onto a greased cookie sheet. Decorate cookies with walnuts, dates, jam or coconut. Bake at 350° F (175° C) for about 20 minutes.

*Coconut Macaroons

5 eggs, beaten
1 cup matzah meal
2 cups coconut, shredded
1 1/2 cups sugar
1/4 tsp. salt
2 lemons, juice and rind

Mix all ingredients together. Drop spoonfuls on a greased sheet. Bake at 325° F (165° C) for 30–40 minutes, or until browned.

Coconut Cookies

3 egg whites, stiffly beaten
2 cups coconut, shredded

1 tsp. wine vinegar
1 cup sugar

Add sugar gradually to beaten egg whites. Fold in coconut. Add vinegar. Place by teaspoonfuls on a lightly greased baking sheet, allowing room for spreading. Bake at 350° F (175° C) for 12 minutes.

Almond Macaroons

4 egg yolks
1 cup sugar
1/2 tsp. almond extract or 1/4
   tsp. nutmeg

2 cups almonds, ground
40 almond halves

Beat yolks, sugar, extract and add ground nuts. Chill 30 minutes. Roll out balls and top each with half an almond. Bake 10 minutes. Yields 40 almond-topped cookies

Raisin and Nut Cookies

2 cups matzah farfel (finely
   broken-up matzahs)
1 cup nuts, finely chopped
2 cups matzah meal
1 cup raisins

1 1/2 cups sugar
4 eggs
1/2 tsp. salt
1 tsp. cinnamon
2/3 cup oil

Mix all ingredients together and bake on greased cookie sheet at 350° F (175° C) for 30 minutes.

Meringues

4 egg whites
1/8 tsp. salt
1 cup sugar

1 tsp. vanilla
1 tsp. wine vinegar

Beat egg whites and salt until frothy. Gradually add 2/3 cup sugar, 2 T. at a time, beating well after each addition. Beat in remaining sugar, vanilla and vinegar. Beat until stiff peaks are formed. Drop spoonfuls onto heavy paper. Bake at 275° F (135° C) for approximately 1 hour or until quite dry, but not browned.

Chocolate Nut Meringues

2 egg whites
1/2 tsp. vanilla
3/4 cup sugar

1/2 cup chocolate, chopped
1/4 cup nuts, chopped

Beat egg whites until stiff, but not dry. Gradually beat in vanilla and sugar. Fold in chocolate and nuts. Bake on baking paper at 250° F (125° C) for 30 minutes.

Fruit-Filled Meringue Cups

3 egg whites
pinch of salt
3/4 cup sugar
1 T. lemon juice

6 canned peach or pear halves
6 tsp. raspberry preserves
1/4 cup walnuts, chopped

Beat egg whites with salt until fluffy. Add sugar slowly. Add lemon juice with last of sugar and beat until smooth. Place well-drained peach or pear halves on an ungreased baking sheet, hollow-side up. Place teaspoon of preserves in each hollow. Cover each half with meringue. Sprinkle with nuts. Bake at 275° F (130° C) for 1 hour or until lightly browned. Serve hot or cold.

Fruit-Filled Chremsels

Dough:

1 cup water
1/2 cup hot oil
12 oz. (300 g.) matzah meal
5 oz. (130 g.) sugar

3 eggs
1/2 tsp. salt
dash ginger, cinnamon or
   cloves

Combine matzah meal and sugar. Boil water with oil and pour over the matzah meal mixture. Set aside for 30 minutes. Add one egg at a time and beat. Add salt and spices. Form into flat cakes.

Filling:

14 oz. (350 g.) fruit preserves
8 T. chopped nuts

1-2 T. matzah meal

Mix preserves and nuts. Add enough matzah meal so mixture is not runny. Put a spoonful of filling on each cake and fold in half. Fry in hot oil until golden.

*Chremsels

2 cups matzah meal	1 cup water
1 tsp. salt	1/2 cup oil
1 T. sugar	4 eggs

Combine matzah meal, salt and pepper. Add sugar. Bring oil and water to a boil. Add to matzah meal and mix well. Add eggs, one at a time and mix well. Oil hands and shape into patties. Place on well-greased cookie sheet and bake for 50 minutes at 375°F (190° C).

Pesach Brownies

1 cup oil	1/2 cup walnuts
4 eggs	1 tsp. vanilla sugar
2 cups sugar	or 1 tsp. vanilla
1/2 cup potato starch	1/2 cup cocoa

Mix all ingredients and pour into lightly-greased baking dish. Bake at 350° F (175° C) for 30 minutes.

*Easy Brownies

2 eggs	1/2 cup matzah meal
1 cup sugar	5 1/2 T. cocoa
1/4 cup oil	

Beat eggs and sugar. Add all the ingredients gradually and continue mixing. Bake 20 minutes at 325° F (160° C).

*Chocolate Bars

3 eggs	1 cup semi-sweet chocolate
1 cup sugar	1/2 cup nuts, chopped
1/2 cup oil	2 tsp. grated orange peel
3 T. water	1/4 tsp. salt
2 cups matzah meal	

Beat eggs and sugar until thick and lemon colored. Beat in oil and water. Stir in chopped nuts, grated chocolate, orange peel and salt. Add matzah meal and mix well. Let batter stand for 10 minutes. Grease baking sheet. Pour batter into deep baking sheet, about 1/2 inch high, and bake in oven at 375° F (190° C) for about 20 minutes. Cut into bars and remove from baking sheet to cool.

*Thumbprint Cookies

1/2 cup oil	3/4 cup matzah cake meal
1/2 cup sugar	1 cup nuts
2 eggs	1 tsp. lemon juice

Mix all the ingredients together. Drop by teaspoonfuls on greased cookie sheet. Make indentation with thumb in center of each cookie. Bake at 350° F (175° C) for 5–8 minutes. Fill indentation with jam.

*Mocha Nut Bars

2 oz. (50 g.) chocolate	1/4 tsp. salt
2 whole eggs	1 T. instant coffee
1/2 cup butter	1/2 cup matzah cake meal
1 cup sugar	

Melt butter together with chocolate. Cool. Beat eggs and sugar, add salt and chocolate-butter mixture. Stir in coffee and cake meal. Pour into a well-greased 9-inch square pan. Sprinkle with nuts on top. Bake at 325° F (160° C) 20–25 minutes. Cut into squares while still warm.

Pesach Muffins

4 eggs, separated	2 T. sugar
3/4 cup potato starch	1/2 tsp. salt
2 T. cold water	grated rind of 1/2 lemon

Beat yolks until light. Add sugar gradually, beating until creamy. Add water and rind. Slowly sift in potato starch. Beat egg whites with salt until stiff. Fold into batter. Fill tins 1/2 full. Bake at 350° F (175° C) for 20 minutes. Makes 1 dozen.

*Potato Cupcakes

2 T. matzah meal	1/2 tsp. salt
1 1/2 cups mashed potatoes, cold	1/8 tsp. pepper
	3 T. oil
3 eggs, well beaten	

Mix ingredients together. Fill muffin tins 1/2 full. Bake at 350° F (175° C) for 15–20 minutes. Serve immediately.

*Jelly Squares

2 eggs
1/2 cup oil or melted
  shortening
1/2 cup cake meal
1/2 cup potato starch

3/4 cup jam
1 cup sugar
1/4 tsp. cinnamon
1 cup nuts, chopped

Mix egg yolks with oil and 1/2 cup sugar for 10 minutes. Stir in matzah meal and potato starch. Pour into ungreased pan. Spread with jam and nuts. Bake 10 minutes at 350° F (175° C). Beat egg whites until stiff, gradually adding 1/2 cup sugar and cinnamon. Spread over mixture and bake 25 minutes more. Cut into squares when cool.

*Easy Passover Bagels

3 cups water
1 cup oil
2 cups matzah meal

6 eggs
1 T. sugar

Boil water with oil. Pour matzah meal into this mixture and let cool. Then add eggs, one at a time, and sugar. Mix well. Wet hands and roll into balls. Place the balls on greased cookie sheet and press thumb into center of each. Bake at 325° F (160° C) until golden brown.

*Chocolate Matzah Bars

3/4 cup butter or oil
6 T. cocoa
6 T. sugar
2 T. brandy (optional)
1 tsp. instant coffee

1/2 tsp. vanilla or almond
  extract
6 matzahs
2 eggs

In saucepan, blend butter or oil, cocoa, sugar, brandy, coffee and flavoring. Once well blended, allow mixture to cool, but remain liquid. Beat in eggs. Pour over matzahs which have been broken up and placed in a 30 x 30-centimeter pan. Refrigerate and cut into squares.

★ Mandelbroit

2 cups matzah meal

4 T. potato starch

1 cup nuts, chopped

4 eggs

1 1/2 cups sugar

1 cup oil

rind of 1/2 lemon

rind of 1/2 orange

Mix dry ingredients. Beat eggs until foamy. Add sugar and mix. Add oil, followed by dry ingredients and rinds. Refrigerate for 2 hours or overnight. Roll into 3 long, wide strips. Bake 25 minutes at 325° F (160° C). Slice and lay on sides to toast for 15–20 minutes.

Holiday Desserts

―――――――――――― CANDIES ――――――――――――

Simple Fondant
Milk Chocolate Fudge
Chocolate Fudge
*Pesach Candy
*Farfel Candy
Almond Chocolate Candy
Nut Brittle
Chocolate Nut Clusters
Nut Candy

Coconut Ice
Carrot Candy
Delicious Dried Apple Slices
Dried Fruit Sweets
Grapefruit Candy
Easy Stuffed Dates
Special Stuffed Dates
Date-Nut Candies

――――――――― FRUIT AND WHIPPED DESSERTS ―――――――――

*Pesach Fruit Kneidlach Dessert
Fruit Salad
Baked Apples
Apple Compote
Baked Apple Compote
Applesauce
Applesauce in the Oven
Banana Dessert
Fried Bananas

Apple Fritters
Rhubarb Dessert
Baked Custard
Truffle Creme
Chocolate Mousse
Chocolate Pudding
Chocolate Cream Dessert
Homemade Lemonade

――――――――――― FROZEN DESSERTS ―――――――――――

Strawberry Fluff
Strawberry Ice
Lemon Ice
Denah's Super Duper Fruit Ice
Vella's Strawberry Sherbet

Coconut Ice Cream
Mommy's Super Pareve Ice Cream
Selma's Delicious Pareve Ice Cream
Frozen Banana Delight

――――――――― FROSTINGS, SAUCES, AND MORE ―――――――――

Honey Frosting
Fluffy Honey Frosting
Mocha Icing
**Chocolate Frosting or Chocolate
  Matzahs*
Mock Whipped Cream

Charoses Sauce
Wine Sauce
Fruit Sauce
Sour Cream Dessert Sauce
Strawberry Jam

Candies

Simple Fondant

10 oz. (250 g.) confectioner's
  sugar or regular sugar
1 egg white
nuts, chopped or whole

flavoring: 1/2 tsp. coffee or
  1 tsp. lemon juice or
  1 tsp. chopped fresh mint

Whip egg white until frothy. Gradually work in sugar. Add flavoring. Add more sugar, if necessary, to get a firm and dry dough. Roll out. Put on greased pan. Cut into squares or rounds. Decorate with nuts. When dry, place in paper cupcake holders.

Milk Chocolate Fudge

1 lb. 2 oz. (450 g.) sugar
5 oz. (125 g.) butter
1 1/2 cups milk

4 oz. (100 g.) sweet chocolate
2 T. honey

Put sugar, butter, milk, chocolate and honey in pan. Heat gently until sugar dissolves. Grease pan. Bring mixture to boil, stirring constantly. Boil fast for 15 minutes, being careful it doesn't boil over. Test that it has reached the "soft ball stage." This means dropping a bit of it into a glass of cold water to see if it forms a ball. Remove pan from heat. Let stand on cool surface for 5 minutes. Beat mixture with spoon until rough and thick. Pour into greased pan. Cool. Cut into squares.

Chocolate Fudge

5 eggs, separated
7 T. sugar
2 cups ground nuts

4 oz. (100 g.) bittersweet
  chocolate
7 T. additional sugar
1 1/2 cups oil

Preheat oven to 375° F (190° C). Beat egg whites until stiff. Add sugar and beat while adding nuts. Place mixture in pan. Bake until golden brown. Melt chocolate in a baking dish in oven. Mix yolks and add additional sugar. Add oil and mix well. Continue blending while adding melted chocolate. Pour over first mixture in pan. Bake 10 minutes maximum. Cool and refrigerate.

*Pesach Candy

1 tsp. ginger	*1 cup sugar*
1 tsp. cinnamon	*matzah meal to thicken*
1 cup honey	

Melt sugar over low flame, stirring constantly. Add honey. Simmer very slowly for 3 minutes. Add spices and matzah meal. Pour onto greased surface. Cut into squares.

*Farfel Candy

1 lb. 4 oz. (1/2 K.) honey	*3/4 cup matzah farfel (or*
1/4 cup sugar	*finely chopped matzahs)*
3 cups nuts, chopped	

Boil honey and sugar until brown. Slowly mix in farfel and nuts. Cool until thick. Pour into large, greased pan. Wet hands with ice water and pat candy to 3/4 inch thickness. Let cool and cut into desired shapes.

Almond Chocolate Candy

1 cup almonds	*4 oz. (100 g.) sweet chocolate*
1/2 cup sugar	*1 T. water*
2 egg yolks	

Grind nuts. Grate chocolate and add 1/2 of chocolate to almonds. Add egg yolks, water and sugar. Blend into firm paste. Shape into balls and roll in remaining grated chocolate. Place on cookie sheet in refrigerator or other cool place for 5 hours.

Nut Brittle

1 lb. (1/2 K.) mixed nuts	*2 cups sugar*

Cook sugar in heavy frying pan on low flame until it turns to liquid. Mix in chopped nuts. Pour onto foil. Allow to harden. Break into pieces.

Chocolate Nut Clusters

6 oz. (150 g.) semi-sweet chocolate	*1 1/2 cups walnuts, chopped*

Melt chocolate over warm water in double boiler. Stir in chopped walnuts. Drop by teaspoonfuls on wax paper and chill.

Nut Candy

2 cups honey
1/2 cup sugar

1 lb. (1/2 K.) nuts, finely
   chopped

Boil honey and sugar for 10 minutes. Slowly add nuts. Cook until thick. Pour into large, greased pan. Pat with cold wet hands until 1-inch thick. Cut with sharp knife.

Coconut Ice

1 lb. (400 g.) sugar
1/3 cup water (may need a little more)

4 oz. (100 g.) coconut

Heat sugar and water slowly in pan until dissolved. Boil for 3 minutes. Test that it has reached the "soft ball stage." This means dropping a bit of it into a glass of cold water to see if it forms a ball. Remove from stove. Mix with coconut. When thick, put in pan, cool and cut. Fattening, but really good!

Carrot Candy

1 lb. 4 oz. (1/2 K.) carrots,
   cooked
little less than 1 lb. (1/2 K.)
   sugar
1/2 cup orange juice

1/2 tsp. salt
3 oz. (75 g.) almonds, ground
1 tsp. ginger
1 tsp. vanilla

Mash carrots through strainer. Pour off juice. Add rest of ingredients. Cook on a low flame for 30 minutes or until thick. Stir often to prevent burning. Sprinkle a little sugar and ginger on a board. Spread mixture. Sprinkle more sugar and ginger. Cool. Cut before it gets hard.

Delicious Dried Apple Slices

2 lb. (1 K.) apples, peeled   sugar and cinnamon

Cut aluminum foil to fit large pan. Cover foil with sugar and cinnamon. Slice apples thick. Spread on sugared foil. Place in oven with only pilot light on. Leave for 1 day. Turn over once.

Dried Fruit Sweets

20 dates
2 oz. (50 g.) raisins
10 prunes
2 oz. (50 g.) nuts, grated
juice of 1 lemon

lemon peel, grated
cinnamon and ginger, to taste
2 oz. (50g.) coconut or
2 oz. (50 g.) additional nuts,
grated

Pit dried fruits. Scald by pouring boiling water over them. Grind. Add other ingredients, except coconut or additional nuts. Mix and knead mixture. Shape into balls. Roll in remaining nuts or coconut.

Grapefruit Candy

3 grapefruit rinds   2 lbs. (1 K.) sugar

Cut grapefruit rind into strips or small triangles, removing most of white from peel. Boil in water 5 minutes. Drain. Repeat 2 or 3 more times until peel is tender. Drain well, squeezing out as much water as possible. Make a syrup from sugar and 1/2 cup water. Bring to a boil and place the peel in syrup. Allow to boil until syrup is absorbed (peel is glazed), but do not allow grapefruit rinds to become dry. Remove from fire. Place on a wet board for a few minutes. Roll rinds in granulated sugar.

Easy Stuffed Dates

Remove pits carefully from dates by slicing one side. Put a whole almond into each. Close up. Roll in confectioner's sugar or coconut. Delicious!

Special Stuffed Dates

2 oz. (50 g.) confectioner's
  sugar
2 oz. (50 g.) almonds, ground

1 egg white
1/2 lb. (200 g.) dates

Mix sugar and almonds. Whip egg white until frothy. Add to sugar mixture. Knead until smooth and firm. Add more sugar, if necessary. Slit dates. Remove pits. Shape almond paste into tiny sausages and place inside each date.

Date-Nut Candies

1/2 lb. (200 g.) pitted dates   *1 egg white*
1/2 lb. (200 g.) walnuts   *2 T. sugar*

Chop dates and walnuts. Roll in shape of date. Refrigerate for 2 hours until set. Beat egg white a little, adding sugar. Dip each date-nut candy into this coating. Place on greased pan. Bake at 350° F (175° C) until crisp.

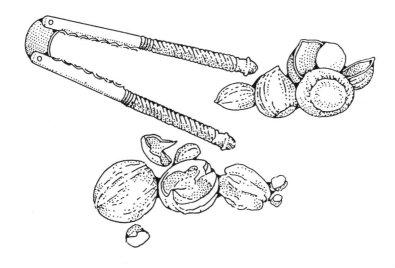

Fruit and Whipped Desserts

★Pesach Fruit Kneidlach Dessert

1 lb. (400 g.) prunes
2 slices lemon
3 eggs, separated
1/2 tsp. salt

3 T. oil
3/4 cup matzah meal
almonds

Wash prunes and soak overnight in water to cover. Next day, simmer prunes in the same water with lemon slices. Meanwhile, prepare kneidlach. Beat egg whites until stiff. Add beaten egg yolks, salt, oil and matzah meal. Mix well. Form into balls about the size of a walnut, inserting an almond into the center of each. Sweeten prunes to taste. Place the kneidlach in a casserole dish. Pour the prunes and juice over them. Bake in a moderate oven 350° F (175° C) for 30 minutes. Serves 4–6.

Fruit Salad

2 oranges, peeled and cut up
3 bananas
a few dates

a few drops of wine
lemon juice

Slice bananas and pour lemon juice over them. Combine all ingredients, mix and serve.

Baked Apples

6 apples
1/2 tsp. cinnamon

1/3 cup sugar or sweetener

Wash and core apples. Make a slit in skin around each apple. Place apples on greased baking dish. Mix cinnamon with sugar or sweetener. Fill centers. Bake 1 hour at 375° F (190° C).

Apple Compote

1 lb. (1/2 K.) apples
2 cups water

sugar, to taste
juice of 1 lemon

Core apples. Cut into quarters or circles. Put apples and water in a pot. Bring to boil and simmer for 30 minutes. Add sugar and lemon to taste. Cool and serve.

Baked Apple Compote

8 apples	4 whole cloves
2/3 cup red wine	1/8 tsp. salt
2/3 cup sugar	1/2 lemon, sliced
1 tsp. cinnamon	

Place whole apples in wonder pot. Combine wine, sugar, cinnamon, cloves, salt and lemon. Pour sauce over apples. Bake until tender, basting frequently.

Applesauce

4 1/2 lb. (2 K.) cooking apples, unpeeled and cored	juice of 1/2 lemon
	sugar, to taste
orange juice	

Cover with water and cook apples until water boils. Remove from flame. When somewhat cooled, mash and add immediately the juice of 1/2 lemon. Add orange juice and sugar to taste.

Applesauce in the Oven

6–8 tart apples	2/3 cup water
cinnamon to taste or	3/4 cup sugar
2 thin slices lemon	

Wash apples (do not peel) and cut into quarters. Place in baking dish. Add cinnamon or lemon and water. Cover and bake at 375° F (190° C) until tender, approximately 30 minutes. Push through a strainer. Add sugar and mix.

Banana Dessert

4 ripe bananas, sliced thin	1 T. lemon juice
2 cups orange or grapefruit juice	1/2 cup dates, finely chopped

Mix juices. Add to bananas and dates. Mix.

Fried Bananas

bananas	white sugar
oil	red wine

Roll peeled and sliced bananas in sugar. Sprinkle with wine. Fry about 5 minutes in oil. Serve hot.

Apple Fritters

16 sliced apple rings, 1/4-inch thick
8 eggs
8 T. cold water
2 T. potato starch
1/2 tsp. salt
1/4 cup sugar

Dissolve starch in water and add rest of ingredients, ex apple rings. Heat oil in heavy pan. Dip apple rings in n and fry over medium heat on both sides until golden b

Rhubarb Dessert

2 lb. (1 K.) rhubarb
1 cup fresh pineapple
2 cups strawberries
sugar, to taste

Cook rhubarb (with very little water). When almost tender, add 1 cup fresh pineapple cut into chunks and cook 5 minutes longer. Add 2 cups strawberries and sugar — approximately 1 cup. Cook 2 more minutes. Refrigerate.

Baked Custard

4 egg yolks, lightly beaten
4 cups milk
2 T. sugar
1 tsp. vanilla extract
dash cinnamon

Using small bowl, combine all ingredients except cinnamon. Stir until well blended. Pour mixture into 4 custard cups. Sprinkle with cinnamon. Set custard cups in baking pan filled with about 1/2 inch of hot water. Bake about 1 hour at 325° F (165° C). Let cool, then chill in refrigerator.

Truffle Creme

6–8 oz. (150–200 g.) semi-sweet chocolate
3 egg yolks
3 egg whites, stiffly beaten
1 T. lemon juice or wine
1 T. sugar
2/3 cup apple juice

Melt chocolate in dish over saucepan. Remove from stove. Fold in egg yolks. Stir. Add sugar, lemon juice (or wine) and the stiffly beaten whites. Refrigerate in individual dishes or in serving dish.

Aish HaTorah

- •Igniting Jewish pride
- •Deepening Jewish awareness
- •Uniting the Jewish people

Aish HaTorah World Center directly behind the Western Wall

More than any other time, visitors to the Western Wall are open to their Jewishness and spirituality. They are wondering: Who are the Jewish People? What is our destiny? People have an experience but don't know how to articulate it. Aish HaTorah is there at the Western Wall to give each individual an understanding of the power of being Jewish.

Aish HaTorah – What We Do

Yeshivat Aish HaTorah - Jerusalem@Aish.edu
Full-time, intensive study program for men. Levels range from beginner to rabbinical ordination.

EYAHT - Eyaht@Aish.edu
Aish HaTorah's College of Jewish Studies for Women. Explores the depth of Jewish thought and practice, while unlocking the potential of the Jewish woman.

Essentials - Essentials@Aish.edu
Jewel - Jewel@Aish.edu
Introductory programs for men and women, ages 18-30. Students can drop in for a class, a day, a week or a month to hear classes from leading experts on Jewish thought.

JEWEL (Jewish Women's Educational League) - Womenorg@netvision.net.il
Supports and organizes educational seminars and social events bringing together Jewish women from a wide variety of backgrounds. Publications include *The Taste of Shabbos Cookbook* and *The Kosher for Passover Cookbook*, both published by Feldheim.

Discovery Seminars - Discovery.USA@Aish.edu
Discovery uses scientific methods of research to explore the authenticity of Judaism and its relevance today. The Discovery Seminar series includes: Crash Course in Jewish History; Love, Dating and Marriage; Why the Jews? (roots of antisemitism); WorldPerfect (the Jewish contribution to humanity); and the Zenith Express (Judaism and the pursuit of pleasure).

Jerusalem Fellowships - JF@Aish.edu
A hand-picked group of talented young people spend one month in Israel in a program that strengthens commitment to Judaism through an intellectual and experiential exploration of Jewish philosophy, history and Israeli politics. Groups come from North America, England, South Africa, Australia, Chile and Russia - as well as native Israelis.

AISH HATORAH AROUND THE WORLD

E.L.C. (Executive Learning Center) - ELC@Aish.edu
E.L.C. provides visitors to Jerusalem with learning and touring programs designed for executives and professionals. Each schedule is tailor-made. Classes are held in Aish HaTorah's World Center, located opposite the Western Wall.

Missions - Missions@Aish.edu
Specialized touring and learning in Israel for groups of singles, families and VIP's to learn, grow and rediscover Judaism in the land of our heritage.

The Russian Program - Russian@Aish.edu
Teacher training program in Israel produces leaders to staff our 10 outreach centers throughout the former Soviet Union, leading the effort to revive Jewish heritage for hundreds of thousands of Russian Jews. Programs in Israel include RETURN, which helps immigrants step-by-step successfully integrate into Israeli society.

Voices from Jerusalem - Voices@Aish.edu
Over 2,000 Torah cassettes from which to choose. The Aish audio collection offers the best Jewish speakers, with the convenience of learning at your own level and pace.

Internet Website - Webmaster@Aish.edu
Your gateway to Aish HaTorah's international network of learning and inspiration. Features 24-hour live pictures of the Western Wall from a camera mounted atop the new Aish HaTorah World Center. Offers email lists on topics from spirituality to relationships to current issues.

Branches
Local programming in 32 cities on five continents. Seminars, single events, executive learning groups, Shabbat programs and more. See listings on the following pages for the branch closest to you.

AISH HATORAH AROUND THE WORLD

ISRAEL

AISH HATORAH WORLD CENTER
1 WesternWall Plaza
P.O.B. 14149
Old City, Jerusalem
Tel: (972-2) 628-5666
Fax: (972-2) 627-3172
Email: Jerusalem@Aish.edu
website:http://www.aish.edu

THE DISCOVERY CENTER
70 Misgav Ladach
Old City, Jerusalem
Tel: (972-2) 627-2355
Fax: (972-2) 627-7742
Email:Discovery.Israel@Aish.edu

JERUSALEM FELLOWSHIPS
P.O.B 14149
Old City, Jerusalem 91141
Tel: (972-2) 628-3879
Fax: (972-2) 626-4050
Email: JF.Israel@Aish.edu

EYAHT-Aish HaTorah College for Women
22 Imrei Bina
Kiryat Sanz, Jerusalem
Tel: (972-2) 538-2522
Fax: (972-2) 537-4163
Email: Eyaht@Aish.edu

Rabbi Noach Weinberg, Rosh Yeshiva of Aish HaTorah, and Rebbetzin Dina Weinberg

JEWEL-Jewish Women's Education League
POB259
Kiryat Yearim
Harei Yehuda, Jerusalem
Tel: (972-2) 533-2144
Fax: (972-2) 533-6360
Email: womenorg@netvision.net.il

AISH HATORAH AROUND THE WORLD

CHILE

SANTIAGO
1008 Holanda, Apt. 602
Providencia, Santiago
Tel: (562) 232-8484
Fax: (562) 334-3951
Email: Chile@Aish.edu

ENGLAND

LONDON
9 Arkleigh Mansions
200 Brent St. London
England NW41BH
Tel: (44-181)202-8234
Fax: (44-181)202-8245
Email: England@Aish.edu

SOUTH AFRICA

JOHANNESBURG
32 Aida Avenue, PO Box 26
Cyrildene, Johannesburg
South Africa
Tel: (27-11) 616-3312
Fax: (27-11) 622-7463
Email: Joburg@Aish.edu

AUSTRALIA

MELBOURNE
3/61 Hotham St.
East St. Kilda
3183 Victoria Australia
Tel: (613-9) 525-9456
Fax: (613-9) 527-4769
Email: Australia@Aish.edu

CANADA

TORONTO
949 Clark Avenue West
Thornhill, Ontario L4J 8G6
Tel: (905) 764-1818
Fax: (905) 764-1606
Email: Toronto@Aish.edu

AISH HATORAH AROUND THE WORLD

UNITED STATES

BOSTON, MASSACHUSETTS
77 Englewood Avenue
Brookline, MA 02146
Tel: (617) 731-1324
Fax: (617) 731-0037
Email: Boston@Aish.edu

CLEVELAND, OHIO
14055 Cedar Road, Suite 309
South Euclid, OH 44188
Tel: (216) 321-7277
Fax: (216) 321-8844
Email: Cleveland@Aish.edu

DETROIT, MICHIGAN
32751 Franklin Road
Franklin, MI 48025
Tel: (810) 737-0400
Fax: (810) 737-0405
Email: Detroit@Aish.edu

DISCOVERY USA
805 Kings Highway
Brooklyn, NY 11223
Tel: (718) 376-2775
Fax: (718) 376-2702
Email: Discovery.USA@Aish.edu

JERUSALEM FUND, INC.
3414 Prairie Avenue
Miami Beach, FL 33140
Tel: (305) 535-2474
Fax: (305) 531-9334
Email: JeruFundMI@Aish.edu

LAKEWOOD, NEW JERSEY
24 Davis Road
Lakewood, NJ 08701
Tel: (908) 364-4770
Fax: (908) 367-7142

LOS ANGELES, CALIFORNIA
1417 S. Doheny Drive
Los Angeles, CA 90035
Tel: (310) 278-8672
Fax: (310) 278-6925
Email: LA@Aish.edu

AISH HATORAH AROUND THE WORLD

MIAMI, FLORIDA
1055 NE Miami Gardens Drive
N. Miami Beach, FL 33179
Tel: (305) 945-2155
Fax: (305) 945-6790
Email: Miami@Aish.edu

NEW YORK, NEW YORK
313 West 83rd Street
New York, New York 10024
Tel: (212) 579-1388
Fax: (212) 579-1387
Email: NY@Aish.edu

NORTH AMERICAN JERUSALEM FELLOWSHIPS
2124 Broadway, Suite 224
New York, NY 10023
Tel: (212) 643-8802
Fax: (914) 425-8442
Email: JF@Aish.edu

PHILADELPHIA, PENNSYLVANIA
Kaiserman Jewish
Community Center
45 Haverford Road, Wynnewood PA
19096
Tel: (610) 896-2400
Fax: (610) 896-9770
Email:Phila@Aish.edu

ST. LOUIS, MISSOURI
8149 Delmar Boulevard
St. Louis, MO. 63130
Tel: (314) 862-2474
Fax: (314) 862-4643
Email: StLouis@Aish.edu

WASHINGTON D.C.
11618 Seven Locks Road
Potomac, MD 20854
Tel: (301) 983-1959
Fax: (301) 299-4370
Email: Washington@Aish.edu

COMMONWEALTH OF INDEPENDENT STATES (CIS)

MOSCOW
8 Pokrovsky Boulevard,
Bldg 2, Apt.22, Moscow,Russia
Tel/Fax: (7-095) 917-9592
Email: Moscow@Aish.edu

AISH HATORAH AROUND THE WORLD

ST. PETERSBURG
17/93 Bolotnaya St.
St. Petersberg, Russia
Tel/Fax: (7-812) 552-0414
Email: St.Petersburg@Aish.edu

KIEV
19/10 Pushkinskaya St.
Kiev, Russia
Tel/Fax: (380-44) 224-6860
Email: Kiev@Aish.edu

MINSK
23 Grekova
Minks, Belarus
Tel: (375-172) 466-521/71/11
Fax: (375-172) 323-147
Email: Minsk@Aish.edu